The Animal Part

The Animal Part

HUMAN AND OTHER ANIMALS IN THE POETIC IMAGINATION

Mark Payne

The University of Chicago Press   CHICAGO & LONDON

The University of Chicago Press, Chicago 60637
The University of Chicago Press, Ltd., London
© 2010 by The University of Chicago
All rights reserved. Published 2010.
Paperback edition 2015
Printed and bound by CPI Group (UK) Ltd, Croydon, CR0 4YY

24 23 22 21 20 19 18 17 16 15   2 3 4 5 6

ISBN-13: 978-0-226-65084-5 (cloth)
ISBN-13: 978-0-226-27232-0 (paper)
ISBN-13: 978-0-226-65085-2 (e-book)
10.7208/chicago/9780226650852.001.0001

Library of Congress Cataloging-in-Publication Data

Payne, Mark (Mark Edward)
The animal part : human and other animals in the poetic imagination /
Mark Payne.
p. cm.
Includes bibliographical references and index.
ISBN-13: 978-0-226-65084-5 (cloth : alk. paper)
ISBN-10: 0-226-65084-7 (cloth : alk. paper) 1. Animals in literature.
2. Philosophical anthropology in literature. I. Title.
PN56.A64P39 2010
809'.93362—dc22
2009046954

♾ This paper meets the requirements of ANSI/NISO z39.48-1992
(Permanence of Paper).

FOR LAURA AND BABY CAROLYN, WHO DON'T NEED
JACK KEROUAC TO REMIND THEM
"THE GREAT REQUIREMENT IS A LOVING HEART"

CONTENTS

ACKNOWLEDGMENTS

I would like to thank my colleagues at the University of Chicago who read early versions of this manuscript. Danielle Allen, Elizabeth Asmis, Robert von Hallberg, Oren Izenberg, Heather Keenleyside, Sarah Nooter, Joshua Scodel, and Richard Strier have all made this book better than it would have been without them. To David Wray I owe special thanks for the weekly talks that nourished the work at every stage in its development. I would also like to thank the members of the university's Poetry and Poetics workshop for their comments on an early version of chapter 1, and the members of my spring 2009 class on Aristophanes' *Birds* for their astute commentary both on the play and my thoughts about it. I am grateful to the Franke Institute for the Humanities for a faculty fellowship in 2007 that afforded me an opportunity for continuous labor I would not otherwise have had. Finally, I would like to thank Alan Thomas of the University of Chicago Press for his support, and the press readers for comments that were of immense value to me in preparing this work for publication.

Imagining Animals

A BEAVER AND A FOX

Kingston Lake Campground, site no. 11, Pictured Rocks National Lakeshore, Michigan, July 2006. I have driven from Chicago to the upper peninsula of Michigan. After driving around the dirt roads that intersect the backcountry of the Lake Superior shoreline, I settle on a campground by a small inland lake. I pitch my tent under some pine trees in the back of a secluded lot. The fire pit and eating area are in front of me, and from there, a path down to a small sandy beach with a view across to an island with an impressive stand of bigger pines. I'm hot from the drive so I swim over and back.

The next day I walk to Lake Superior along the Fox River Trail, which is dry, sandy, and very hot. At about the half-way point, I reach Kettle Hole Lake where a single heron is poking around. It's four miles each way to Lake Superior and when I get back in the evening I drink four beers waiting for the stars. A toad hops into my flashlight. There's a thunderstorm from 4:30 a.m. to 8:00 or so, in two waves of lightning, enormous crashes, and driving rain. Happily, my tent holds up.

On Sunday I walk to Chapel Falls and Chapel Beach, then along the Lake Superior trail to Mosquito River and Mosquito Beach. I hang my clothes on a big camp of old driftwood and swim. Walking back I wave to sightseeing boats from the tops of cliffs and feel a strange urge to leap from the overhanging ledges (vertigo?). I marvel at the single pine tree that clings to Chapel Rock, a sandstone bluff weathered into twisting columns and flutes (a white pine, as I learn from Pamela Baker, a park ranger who answers the question I post on the ParkNet Web site after I return home).

On Sunday night almost everyone is gone from the campground. As I sit in my folding chair drinking beer and waiting for the sunset once again, I spot a big "V" of raised water speeding across the lake to where I am sitting. I get up out of my chair and see about one-third of a squarish head sticking out of the water. I've never seen one before, but I know it must be a beaver. As he gets closer—I think *he* for reasons that will become clear—it looks like he wants to come ashore but the few people remaining at the campground are putting him off. Instead of turning around, however, he swims in long ellipses parallel to the shore, going back and forth for ten to fifteen minutes as I attempt to keep pace with him through the mud and bushes at the edge of the lake. Eventually he gives up and swims off in a different direction.

What strikes me is how preoccupied he seems. His rapid unswerving path across the lake is full of purpose, as if he was coming to accomplish something, and the elliptical movement he adopts on not being able to land suggests frustration, as if he couldn't quite relinquish the task he had set himself. I am reminded of days I can't find a book I want in the library. For a while I go back and forth along the stacks in vain, unwilling to give up on my reading plan, before eventually resigning myself to the fact that the book isn't there and that there are, after all, other books I could be reading. The beaver, I think, in his single-minded devotion to the job in hand, is an animal pursuing his distinctive occupations; I too am one. His activity is not a symbol or image of mine, it is a behavior we share.

After a few more days in the UP I drive back to Chicago through the North Woods of Wisconsin. As I pass through the small roadside towns I wonder, not entirely ironically now, why so many have chosen to emblematize themselves in the form of gigantic fiberglass animals that loom over the highway, bigger than people. Why is every front yard crowded with plastic birds and deer? What is being asserted here? Mostly, though, I'm thinking about a childhood experience with my grandfather, one that I've never stopped thinking about, off and on, for years, but which now returns with insistence. One year at the end of summer, we had gone shooting to a wheat field that had been cut from the outside in, leaving a small square of standing crops in the center. Along with a few farm workers, we positioned ourselves around this square to shoot whatever animals had retreated into it as the field was cut, and would now be driven out by beating what remained of the wheat with sticks.

We expected rabbits, but, at the corner where I was posted, a fox ran out instead. My grandfather raised pheasants for shooting and was not concerned about saving foxes for hunting with horse and hounds. As I raised my gun, however, the fox stopped dead in its tracks and looked at me without moving. I do not know if this was a defensive strategy, or if it was just surprised to see me, but I do know that if it had tried to run to the woods at the edge of the field without stopping I would have killed it. Now I could not pull the trigger, and it trotted away to safety almost casually.

THE HUNTER BECOMES THE HAUNTED

I had shot plenty of animals before, wrung the necks of rabbits and pigeons, and even seen a furious fox writhe on a bloody leg that had somehow got entangled in a barbed wire fence before being dispatched from close range. This time, however, the animal had made contact with me. I had looked into its eyes, and I knew that it was looking at me, and that it knew that I knew. What I didn't know then is that there is an archive of hunting narratives that focus on this moment of eye contact between hunter and hunted. Perhaps the most famous modern example, and certainly the most influential, is the death of the wolf in Aldo Leopold's *A Sand County Almanac*. In the section entitled "Thinking like a Mountain," Leopold describes an experience early in his career when, as a park ranger in Arizona, he and some colleagues shot and killed a large female wolf they had seen fording a mountain river with her pups:

> We reached the old wolf in time to watch a fierce green fire dying in her eyes. I realized then, and have known ever since, that there was some- thing new to me in those eyes—something known only to her and to the mountain. I was young then, and full of trigger-itch; I thought that because fewer wolves meant more deer, that no wolves would mean hunters' paradise. But after seeing the green fire die, I sensed that nei- ther the wolf nor the mountain agreed with such a view.[1]

Leopold has an argument for wolves: loss of predators means too many deer, which in turn leads to deforestation and starvation among the deer themselves. The argument does not, however, originate in such rational calcu- lations but in the encounter with a particular animal. In the experience of the wolf's eyes, Leopold understands what its life is for itself, as a creature at the center of its own web of belonging and its attendant concerns. To have under-

---

1. Leopold 1949, 130.

stood this is "to think like a mountain," because only the mountain has been around long enough to perceive each of its inhabitants on its own terms.

The ecological argument is founded on empathetic imagination: not only is this its origin, it also proves to be the best way of grasping the complexity of the local situation. To be asked to think like a mountain moves the question of the imagination far beyond any anxieties we might feel about projecting human concerns onto, or into, other animals, and toward the effort to imagine the totality of life at hand. And what Leopold tells us is that a muted version of such imagining is going on inside us all the time. It is the felt presence of our surroundings that we seldom try to articulate as conscious experience: "Only the ineducable tyro can fail to sense the presence or absence of wolves, or the fact that mountains have a secret opinion about them."[2]

As Leopold describes it, looking into the dying wolf's eyes was the experience that precipitated his own emergence from background awareness into conscious imagining, a life of writing that endeavored to make the deep furrow of sensibility churned by the wolf's death bear fruit as discourse and persuasion. It would not be wrong to describe "Thinking like a Mountain" as a conversion narrative: two versions of a self lie on either side of an experience that divides them, and a sacrifice enables the passage from one to the other.

It is as a conversion narrative struggling to achieve resolution that Ernest Hemingway's hunting fiction, "An African Story," takes shape.[3] The story begins with its narrator, David, remembering the remorse he felt as a child when he betrayed the location of a large bull elephant to his father and the African guide of their hunting expedition. As they pursue the elephant over the course of several days, the story witnesses the difficult birth of adult consciousness in the child as he tries to keep his sympathy with the animal a secret from the adults he is with. The situation is a perfect double bind: on the one hand, he wants to hide his anger and his tears in order to remain aloof

2. Ibid. Arne Naess has likewise described how seeing guide poles stuck into Hallingskarvet precipitated his understanding of how this mountain was, for him, alive: "To some people, the word *alive* embraces more than the biological sense alone. Hallingskarvet is the only mountain that I feel to be alive. I had a proof of this attitude when I once saw that an extremely long line of green-painted poles had been put out to prevent imbecile tourists from falling down the precipices in winter. It was clear to me that these poles offended Hallingskarvet's *dignity*" (2002, 107; original emphasis).

3. The story appears discontinuously in Hemingway's posthumous novel, *The Garden of Eden*, as an autobiographical narrative its protagonist David struggles to complete. The pieces are excerpted and joined together to form an independent short fiction in *The Complete Short Stories of Ernest Hemingway* (1987, 545–54). I cite this version for convenience, but with the reservations discussed below.

and emotionally inaccessible to the adults he despises; on the other hand, it is the inability to conceal his emotions that makes him unlike them and like the elephant, who, even as they are tracking him, pauses to caress the skull of a companion killed by the hunters on a previous occasion.

As narrator of his own story, David tries to pare away his retrospective feelings about the episode so that he can reproduce exactly what he experienced as a child. In the pursuit phase of the hunt, he thinks of his sorrow for the elephant, as an old animal hunted at the end of its life, as a reflex of his own exhaustion, as a child pressed into an adult task for which he was unsuited. At this stage, then, his sympathy is fundamentally corporeal: two tired creatures are involved against their will in a physical trial. At the killing itself, however, his feelings for the elephant become "love" (551), as, by looking into its eyes, he is able to grasp what the animal's life is for itself:

> They found him anchored in such suffering and despair that he could no longer move . . . He did not move but his eye was alive and looked at David. He had very long eyelashes and his eye was the most alive thing David had ever seen . . . But he didn't look at me as though he wanted to kill me. He only looked sad the same way I felt. He visited his old friend on the day he died. (552–53)

David acknowledges the killing as the decisive moment for his own sense of selfhood, but his name for this moment—"the beginning of the knowledge of loneliness" (553)—points to the difference between his story and Leopold's. For Leopold, the understanding of the dying animal precipitated by looking into its eyes extends outward to a sympathetic vision of a world of striving beings in which he and the wolf are two such beings among others. He is no longer alone, for he has felt the presence of the other inhabitants of his world for the first time. By contrast, David's consciousness becomes intensive: his feelings remain focused upon his father, and barely concealed hostility that expresses his new sense of solitude takes the place of the unreflective emotional proximity that preceded the death of the elephant. Rather than moving outward to the world at large, David's sympathetic feelings are constrained by the aggression toward his father that emerges along with them; the elephant becomes his "hero," "as his father had been for a long time" (553).

In the story David writes, his father is an unsympathetic person incapable of understanding his own response to the elephant. In the passages of the novel that surround it, however, David acknowledges that his father in fact saw and understood quite well that his son had experienced some kind of conversion during the hunt: "His father had known how he had felt about the elephant and that night and in the next few days he had tried if not to convert him to bring him back to the boy he had been before he had come to the knowledge that he hated elephant hunting."[4]

If we try to imagine the scenes that are here condensed into a single sentence, we must remember that David's hostility to his father took the form of concealment, so that if his father was trying to reconvert him, his response is likely to have been not a refusal to be reconverted but a denial that any decisive change had taken place. If we ask ourselves why David does not extend his imagination beyond the scene of its emergence, the answer that suggests itself is that his father preempts his ability to do so: even though his account of David's experience is true, the fact that it comes from his father means David cannot accept and develop it as his own.

What David does instead is to try to refashion the conversion narrative proposed by his father as a myth of election. His father understands what has happened to his child as an experience, something that could happen to anyone under such circumstances, and especially to a child taxed beyond its powers of endurance. As such, he thinks what has happened can be undone by other experiences, or by persuasion. David's resistance is to imagine his experience as a revelation guaranteed to him alone. What happened with the elephant was not a transformative event that could happen to anyone—as it happened to Leopold—but something that could only be seen by him and not by his father. David uses up his imaginative energies fashioning a father who could not see what he has seen, despite the evidence to the contrary. Because he also knows that this father is not real, his imagination remains guilty and solipsistic; he cannot share or extend his sympathetic identification with the elephant, and his work on his story separates him from his partner Catherine, who views it with suspicion.[5]

My last example of "the strange bondage of the eyes" comes from J. A. Baker's *The Peregrine*.[6] Baker's book is not about hunting, but bird watching,

4. Hemingway 1986, 200.

5. Cf. Wolfe (2003b, 142–68), who argues that David's father's foreclosure of his youthful identification with the elephant is the origin of his compensatory cross-gender identification with Catherine. As I see it, it is David's father who kills the elephant but David himself who forecloses his identification with others by his unwillingness to leave the scene of the crime. If he is able to identify with Catherine, it is only at her instigation.

6. Baker (1967, 97). The 2005 reissue by New York Review Books has a fine introduction by Robert Macfarlane that, in addition to a commentary on its place in recent nature writing, supplies the very little that is known about its author.

and it is structured as a conversion narrative in reverse. In Leopold and Hemingway, the eyes of a dying animal compel an unexpected recognition from a human being of what that animal's life has been to it. Baker, by contrast, describes how his obsessive observation of peregrine falcons turned into an attempt to get the individual birds he followed to recognize and acknowledge him not merely as one human being among others, but as a specific individual with particular relations with them. The successful outcome of his quest is recorded in the book's final pages as "the great eyes of the peregrine" look into his without alarm—"as though they see something beyond me from which they cannot look away"—and the falcon allows himself to sleep as Baker stands before him.

What distinguishes Baker's book as nature writing is the remarkable richness of its prose. Baker sees his task as not merely to observe birds, but to register every movement of his own response to them: "Everything I describe took place while I was watching it, but I do not believe that honest observation is enough. The emotion and behaviour of the watcher are also facts, and they must be truthfully recorded" (14). The results, as in this account of an encounter with an owl, are an extraordinary continuum of seeing and imagining:

A chill spread over my face and neck. Three yards away, on a pine branch close to the ride, there was a tawny owl. I held my breath. The owl did not move. I heard every small sound of the wood as though I too were an owl. It looked at the light reflected in my eyes. It waited. Its breast was white, thickly arrowed and speckled with tawny red. The redness passed over the sides of its face and head to form a rufous crown. The helmeted face was pale white, ascetic, half-human, bitter and withdrawn. The eyes were dark, intense, baleful. This helmet effect was grotesque, as though some lost and shrunken knight had withered to an owl. As I looked at those grape-blue eyes, fringed with their fiery gold, the bleak face seemed to crumble back into the dusk; only the eyes lived on. The slow recognition of an enemy came visibly to the owl, passing from the eyes, and spreading over the stony face like a shadow. But it had been startled out of its fear, and even now did not fly at once. Neither of us could bear to look away. Its face was like a mask; macabre, ravaged, sorrowing, like the face of a drowned man. I moved. I could not help it. And the owl suddenly turned its head, shuffled along the branches as though cringing, and flew softly away into the wood. (78–79)

Baker's prose records the living flow of transactional energies between one animal and another. To hear the wood as the owl hears it is not an exercise in projection but a perceptual change brought about by the meeting itself. To see oneself seen is to become aware of oneself as an object of another animal's perception, then as one object among others in this perception, and then, finally, as a participant in an intersubjective encounter as it is experienced by the other subject. Description of the observing animal must include an account of its human describer, because both are in flux in the encounter; language must try to reach both as they are changed by their presence to one another.

Baker enriches the scene of imaginative sympathy by reinvesting the energies released by it: understandings proliferate, knowledge is gained, imagination is unconstrained and generative. What he learns from the owl is what it is to be an animal that lives by stealth and hunting and to be momentarily taken in by the fascination of the eyes of another. The owl's face, "ascetic, half-human, bitter and withdrawn," is that of a knight become one with the forest that was supposed to be the backdrop to his quest—not a Galahad whose purity of purpose allows him to succeed where others before him have failed, but some nameless knight-errant who finds in his heart the emptiness of the forest itself, the freedom from care that becomes a life of predation.

What does the owl learn from Baker? We cannot know for sure, of course, but it looks to Baker as if the bird has momentarily recorded the claims of responsibility and concern that are discovered in the eyes of one to whom we feel ourselves connected, a minimal form of fascination that stops him from taking flight at the first realization of the other's presence. The owl's troubled discovery of interest in his human observer prefigures the acknowledgment that Baker is finally able to wrest from the falcon he pursues so avidly. Both might even be described as incipient conversion narratives, in which nonhuman hunters are for a moment brought to reflect on the modes of engagement made possible by a different kind of life.

FACE TO FACE?

Jacques Derrida, in "The Animal that Therefore I Am," locates a fault line between "poetic thinking" and "philosophical knowledge" in the latter's unwillingness, or inability, to register the experience of being seen by a nonhuman animal. Real thought about animals is for Derrida "what philosophy has, essentially, had to deprive itself of" in its efforts to secure the human subject, so that whatever thinking about them we do have is "poetic thinking" that has either not been concerned to make binding claims about the difference between human beings and other animals, or has actively sought to suspend such claims.[7]

Derrida is especially concerned to particularize talk about animals, to move philosophical discussion from "the animal" as opposed to "the human" toward the experience of individual animals. His own contribution to this movement is a description of the anxiety he feels when being seen, and above all when being seen naked by his cat. As he experiences it, the cat's gaze is "vacant to the extent of being bottomless, at the same time innocent and cruel perhaps, perhaps sensitive and impassive, good and bad, uninterpretable, unreadable, undecideable, abyssal and secret" (381). The equivocations register the shades of uncertainty, insecurity, and even shame induced by the gaze of an animal that withholds itself, and its way of knowing of its human owner, in their encounters.[8]

Awareness of the transactional nature of his encounters with his cat moves Derrida toward the question of language, both how he understands what his cat's looks have to say to him as a kind of speech, and how he might reproduce this experiential understanding in language of his own. What we want, he argues, is neither "a projection that appropriates" nor "an interruption that excludes," for while we have been well schooled in avoiding the former, the latter is no less a form of "violence or stupidity [*bêtise*]" since it deprives the animal "of every power of manifestation, of the desire to manifest *to me* anything at all, and even to manifest to me in some way *its* experience of *my* language, of *my* words and *my* nudity" (387).

In an interview with Jean-Luc Nancy, Derrida expresses frustration at definitions of language that exclude animals from its use, and seeks to reorient discussion of what language is toward the situational event of communication. The communicative event, Derrida argues, is actually what grounds our understanding of language, since without it "there would be no language," and communicative events obviously do not take place only between human beings. Derrida thus seeks to open philosophy up to the "concrete and current problems" in the science of animal language, and to suspend the distinction between animal communication and human language that philosophy has erected and policed.[9]

7. Derrida (2002, 377–82). Derrida does not investigate the kinds of "poetic thinking" enabled by particular literary genres, but this will be one of the tasks of this book.

8. Cf. Kuzniar (2006, 5–8), for whom Derrida's paper is symptomatic of pet owners' melancholy desire for an impossibly complete understanding of their animal companions.

9. Derrida 1991, 116–17.

Can philosophy add anything to the discussion of these problems, or is its contribution limited to the analysis and undoing of its own history? Derrida offers his account of being seen by his cat in the spirit of Baudelaire, whose cat "has no need of words to utter the longest of sentences," and it certainly looks like concrete phenomenological description, a positive response to philosophers whose "discourses are sound and profound" but for whom "everything goes on as if they themselves had never been looked at, and especially not naked, by an animal that addressed them."[10] One of these philosophers is surely Emmanuel Lévinas, whose "onto-theological determination" of the limits of neighborliness Derrida mentions in passing in his interview with Nancy.[11] Derrida asks how "the thinking of responsibility" might not stop at the determination of the neighbor Lévinas has given, but he does not undertake a detailed investigation of how this determination came to exclude other animals, nor does he answer the question whether their exclusion from Lévinas's ethics is one of the essential philosophical aversions of the gaze to which he refers in "The Animal that Therefore I Am."

Certainly Derrida and others are right to note that direct consideration of animals is almost entirely absent from Lévinas's work. The only places where it appears are two minor pieces that stand outside the main body of his writing, an essay called "The Name of a Dog, or Natural Rights," written in 1975, and "The Paradox of Morality," an interview with a group of British graduate students that took place in 1986, in which Lévinas responds to questions addressed to him in advance by them, some of which press him on the possibility of extending his ethics to animals.[12]

In the first, Lévinas tells the story of a dog named Bobby that persisted in greeting him and his fellow interns in a Nazi labor camp, reaffirming their humanity in the midst of its denial by other men. Lévinas calls the dog "the last Kantian in Nazi Germany," but a Kantian "without the brain needed to universalize maxims and drives." As such, Bobby's greeting does not rise to the level of an address, and Lévinas ends by asserting that his "friendly growling" and "animal faith" were "born from the silence of his forefathers on the banks of the Nile."[13]

The claim that the dog's expressiveness, which looks like the externalization of a desire to manifest something to Lévinas and his companions, origi-

---

10. Derrida 2002, 383.
11. Derrida 1991, 116.
12. Lévinas 1988, 168–80.
13. I refer to the translation in Calarco and Atterton (2004, 47–49).

nates in an inherited disinterest in, or incapacity for, communication is even more surprising given that, in the interview, "The Paradox of Morality," Lévinas takes a large view of language as situational communication that includes the silent address of the look:

> I think that the beginning of language is in the face. In a certain way, in its silence, it calls you . . . Language does not begin with the signs that one gives, with words. Language is above all the fact of being addressed . . . which means the saying much more than the said.[14]

If the dog's bark is not to be understood as communication, this is not because it is not made up of words; rather, it is because nothing that comes from a dog can be construed as coming from a face. For to speak of the face of an animal is to project an experience of human interaction onto it such that the term can only have a secondary, or even metaphorical, meaning:

> One cannot entirely refuse the face of an animal . . . Yet the priority here is not found in the animal, but in the human face . . . It is a notion through which man comes to me via a human act different from knowing . . . only afterwards do we discover the face of an animal. (169–72)[15]

Lévinas is willing to consider the possibility that a "specific phenomenological analysis" of the interaction with particular animals might discover the face in these encounters, as it might also in dealings with children. For children, he claims, "are often loved for their animality"; a child "is not suspicious of anything," and its behavior, like that of animals, exhibits an unselfconsciousness adult human beings lack: "He jumps, he walks, he runs, he bites. It's delightful" (172). The strangeness of this formulation reveals how little concrete phenomenological analysis of children and animals Lévinas himself must have done. Was there ever a child who was not suspicious of anything? Was there ever a dog that was this incautious?

It is the very absence of such analysis in Lévinas's work that leaves it open to the kind of meaningful supplementation he himself is able to imagine. In order to provide it, however, one would first have to grasp what, for Lévinas,

---

14. Lévinas 1988, 169–70.

15. Aristotle notes that the Greek word for face, *prosopon*, is used only of human beings, not animals (*History of Animals* 1.8, 491b10), although, as commentators have pointed out, he, or an interpolator, later contradicts this remark and refers to the faces of chameleons and baboons (503a18).

distinguishes human beings from animals and so grounds the experience of the human face. And this is saintliness, the willingness to sacrifice one's own life for the life of another that he believes is unique to humankind. Lévinas is no more ignorant of "concrete and current problems" in zoological research than Derrida; he refers to Darwin in his assertion of human uniqueness, and is careful to distinguish his account of self-sacrifice from forms of familial or species devotion in other animals that might be claimed as biological ancestors, or analogues, of human altruism.[16]

Saintliness, by contrast, is essentially "unreasonable" and nonreciprocal, severed from all considerations of individual reward or group purpose in which significant others appear as extensions or mediations of selfhood. Indeed, it is only by being outside the reciprocal relationships of family and society that human beings are human at all, for it is only then that "I can demand of myself that which I cannot demand of the other." Not only can the claim of the face that motivates self-sacrifice never be a contract, the fully human being who sacrifices himself for the other can look for nothing in the face of the other to motivate his action or guarantee its value:

> The face is not that which is seen . . . There is no evidence with regard to the face . . . Consequently, you could call it generosity; in other terms, it is the moment of faith . . . It is believing that love without reward is valuable. (Lévinas 1988, 176–77)

Self-sacrifice is essentially gratuitous: generosity belongs entirely to the giver and is not motivated by anything concrete about the other. But if the experience of the face is not grounded in the physiognomy that is seen, ethical phenomenology is an imaginative experience, and there seems to be no good reason why it should not happen with animals.[17] And if this is a concession Lévinas would only grant with reluctance, reluctance is itself fundamental to his account of ethical experience. In *Otherwise Than Being*, he describes the emergence of care from complacency as the "coring out" or "denucleation" of an ego sequestered in its own pleasures, "the tearing away of the mouthful of bread from the mouth that tastes in full enjoyment."[18] Without this pain, eth-

16. Cf. Calarco 2004, 183–84.

17. Cf. Calarco: "We do not and cannot know in advance where the face begins and ends, and this non-knowledge should render any and every determination of the limits of responsibility problematic, contestable and questionable" (2004, 184). The question is given practical ethical urgency in Jeffrey Masson's vegan protreptic *The Face on Your Plate*.

18. Lévinas 1981, 73–74.

ics is merely "elevated feelings" and "belles lettres" (64), for without egotism deprivation is merely endurance of lack, not sacrifice. Reluctance belongs to the phenomenology of care, because reluctance is what makes care gratuitous, "an overflowing of sense by non-sense," as the claim of the other wins out over the ego's quite sensible attachment to its own life.

From this perspective, Lévinas's reluctance to extend his ethics to animals by including them in the experience of the face is understandable. All forms of responsibility are painful interruptions of complacency and self-satisfaction that originate unexpectedly in particular situations and are not the outcome of systematic obligations. That animals might be sources of this interruption is certainly not a possibility Lévinas dwells on, but this does not mean that animals must be excluded from extensions of his ethics we might make for ourselves if their account of commitment to human beings is to remain meaningful. That such commitment is likely to be more painful and involve greater reluctance in the case of animals seems obvious, and it is as a conversion narrative that its emergence is told by Leopold and Hemingway.

IMAGINATION, AND AN ARGUMENT FROM A MARGINAL CASE

Hunting stories involve extreme scenarios and they take place outside the cultural situations in which our everyday experience unfolds. For the claim that makes itself felt in them at the death of the animal to become operative in everyday situations, this moment of unwilled empathetic understanding must become the active exercise of the imagination, as it does in Leopold's "thinking like a mountain." The imagination has an important but highly contested place in discussions of the life of animals, and I would like to approach these discussions by identifying two diametrically opposed positions toward it in contemporary debates.

Thomas Nagel, in a well-known paper, "What Is it Like To Be a Bat?," argues that because "our own experience provides the basic material for our imagination," it does not help "to try to imagine that one has webbing on one's arms, which enables one to fly around at dusk and dawn catching insects in one's mouth," since "in so far as I can imagine this (which is not very far), it tells me only what it would be like for *me* to behave as a bat behaves," whereas what I want to know is "what it is like for a *bat* to be a bat."[19] Nagel suggests, perhaps as a provocation, that there is a deliberate procedure to imagining the

19. Nagel 1974, 439.

life of another animal. First, we form a desire to imagine what it is like to be the animal in question. The next step is a kind of nonactualized dressing up in which we imagine attaching some prosthetic to ourselves that mimics the animal's body. Then we think about ourselves in this shabby getup making ridiculous attempts to do what the animal does without it. This is, of course, nothing like imagining anything. No one needs a wooden leg to imagine himself as a pirate, because what you are aspiring to is not the condition of being unable to walk on two legs of flesh and blood, but the particular way of being in the world that comes with the life of a swashbuckler and is conventionally signified by wooden legs and parrots.[20]

Nagel's assertion of impossibility rests on a contrast between successful and unsuccessful imagining. But what would it mean to imagine being a bat or a pirate unsuccessfully? For Nagel it means to not have the perceptual experience of a bat, but this is to not be a bat, not to fail to imagine being one. What we are after is clear, visible, and immediately grasped in the lives of bats and pirates, and getting to it does not require special procedures or specialized knowledge. Nagel looks forward to a time when "an objective phenomenology not dependent on empathy" would allow us "to think about the subjective character of experience without relying on the imagination," and describe it to others in a form those incapable of having it could understand (449). This, however, would be merely to describe how things look or sound to a bat; to animate such descriptions as lived experience requires the empathetic imagination that has no need of them in the first place.[21]

So, at the opposite pole, J. M. Coetzee's Elizabeth Costello offers two major criticisms of Nagel's account of the imagination. First, Nagel is wrong to suggest that to be able to experience bat life we need the sensory equipment of a bat. To be a living bat is "to be full of being," just as to be a living human being

---

20. Cf. Walton: "It is by mandating the imagining of *propositions* that props generate fictional truths . . . But not all fictional worlds are generated by props" (1990, 42–43).

21. So Adam Smith, in the account of sympathy that begins *The Theory of Moral Sentiments*, contrasts the work of the imagination that allows us to put ourselves in the place of the other with the information provided by descriptive observation that is unable to do so: "As we have no immediate experience of what other men feel, we can form no idea of the manner in which they are affected, but by conceiving what we ourselves should feel in the like situation. Though our brother is upon the rack, as long as we ourselves are at our ease, our senses will never inform us of what he suffers. They never did, and never can, carry us beyond our own person, and it is by the imagination only that we can form any conception of what are his sensations" (1.1.1.1–2; 2002, 11–12).

is, so that "being fully a bat is like being fully human."[22] The fact that the bat is full of bat being, and the human full of human being, is a secondary consideration; since we share the ground of our being with all the other animals, thinking our way into the life of any one of them only requires us to extend to them the same imaginative sympathy that we use to think about the lives of other human beings. This is a capacity that people possess, and choose to exercise, in varying degrees; the problem of imagining anything resides in the imagining subject not the subject to be imagined, and what is really at issue is our reluctance to acknowledge how little difference there is between the pains of our own zoological existence and those that we inflict on other animals.

For Elizabeth Costello, there is "no limit to the extent to which we can think ourselves into the being of another," and "no bounds to the sympathetic imagination":

> If I can think my way into the existence of a being who has never existed, then I can think my way into the existence of a bat or a chimpanzee or an oyster, any being with whom I share the substrate of life. (80)

This is her second point of contention with Nagel: to be human is to be involved at every moment in acts of the imagination that can no more be approached with a demand for descriptive accountability than imagining the life of a bat can. To deny that we can imagine the lives of animals, when imagining the life of Napoleon, Emma Bovary, or our dead and distant relatives is something we could not imagine not doing, is to involve oneself in a denial of what it is to be human in the first place. Stanley Cavell makes a similar point in *The Claim of Reason*:

> To withhold, or hedge, our concepts of psychological states from a given creature, on the ground that our criteria cannot reach to the inner life of the creature, is specifically to withhold the source of my idea that living beings are things that feel; it is to withhold myself, to reject my response to anything as a living being; to blank so much as my idea of *having a body*.

22. All citations from the discussion of Nagel can be found in Coetzee (2003, 75–80). There are valuable discussions of the account of the imagination in *Elizabeth Costello* in Kuzniar (2006, 172–79), who connects it with the euthanasia of dogs in Coetzee's *Disgrace*, and in Malamud (2003, 7–9), who raises the question of whether art can substitute for actual animals in enabling imaginative sympathy with them (42).

It is as one living animal to another that the other animal "calls upon me; it calls me out." No one can answer this call for me; "only I" can "reach to the other's (inner) life," by responding to it as to a voice that I recognize.[23]

Nagel chose the bat as his example of nonhuman life because, unlike wasps or flounders (his counterexamples), they are not so far down the phylogenetic tree that people will disbelieve they have experience at all, but, given that they perceive the world primarily by sonar, or echolocation, their way of being in it presents obvious differences from our own: "Even without the benefit of philosophical reflection, anyone who has spent some time in an enclosed space with an excited bat knows what it is like to encounter a fundamentally *alien* form of life." This sentence encapsulates Nagel's position: on the one hand, there is a claim that "philosophical reflection" will reinforce an alienation from other living beings that is somehow already present in prereflective experience; on the other hand, there is an ascription of feeling to the animal that undoes this claim and what follows from it. For in spite of his arguments for the opacity of the bat's experience, Nagel calls it "excited," thereby acknowledging that he felt something of what it was to be the other animal at the moment he encountered it, and has subsequently used "philosophical reflection" to think away whatever was present to him in that moment.[24]

Elizabeth Costello goes beyond the wasp and the flounder in her assertion that the differences between human beings and other animals are no obstacle to our being able to imagine their lives, taking the oyster as her limit case of imaginative possibility. Rachel Carson is one writer who has given careful thought to the special difficulties involved in imagining nonmammalian marine animals,[25] and, in the remainder of this chapter, I would like to focus

---

23. Cavell (1979, 83–84; original emphasis). Cf. the critical discussion of this passage in connection with Nagel and Wittgenstein in Wolfe (2003a, 9–11).

24. Cf. the dialogue between Chuang Tzu and Hui Tzu cited by Doniger in her discussion of the "If I were a horse" method in comparative anthropology: "Chuang Tzu and Hui Tzu had strolled on to the bridge over the Hao, when the former observed, 'See how the minnows are darting about! That is the pleasure of fishes.' 'You not being a fish yourself,' said Hui Tzu, 'how can you possibly know in what consists the pleasure of fishes?' 'And you not being I,' retorted Chuang Tzu, 'how do you know that I do not know?' 'If I, not being you, cannot know what you know,' urged Hui Tzu, 'it follows that you, not being a fish, cannot know in what consists the pleasure of fishes.' 'Let us go back,' said Chuang Tzu, 'to your original question. You asked me how I knew in what consists the pleasure of fishes. Your very question shows that you knew I knew. I knew it from my own feelings on the bridge'" (1988, 76–77).

25. See Carson: "To get the full feeling of what it is like to be a creature of the sea requires the active exercise of the imagination and the temporary abandonment of many human concepts and human yardsticks . . . On the other hand we must not depart too far from the analogy

on efforts to imagine just one of them—the lobster—in order to get a sense of what the willed exercise of imagination involves in the case of an animal whose life is remote from our own.

In "Consider the Lobster," an essay originally written for, and actually published by, *Gourmet* magazine, David Foster Wallace describes a visit to the Maine Lobster Festival in which sympathetic imagination, and the effort to suppress it, loom large.[26] Wallace reproduces the description of the lobster's nervous system provided by the festival's organizers in order to reassure attendees that the animals do not feel pain when they are boiled alive, and he points out its shortcomings from the perspective of more recent neurological research. What he is really interested in, however, is how lobster eaters marshal the claims of comparative neurology against the lobster's manifest aversion to being immersed in boiling water:

> However stuporous a lobster is from the trip home, for instance, it tends to come alarmingly to life when placed in boiling water. If you are tilting it from a container into the steaming kettle, the lobster will sometimes try to cling to the container's sides or even to hook its claws over the kettle's rim like a person trying to keep from going over the edge of a roof. And worse is when the lobster's fully immersed. Even if you cover the kettle and turn away, you can usually hear the cover rattling and clanking as the lobster tries to push it off. Or the creature's claws scraping the sides of the kettle as it thrashes around. The lobster, in other words, behaves very much as you or I would behave if we were plunged into boiling water. (248)

The discomfort felt when watching a lobster being cooked emerges from sympathetic identification with its behavior, and withholding the response that originates in the shared ground of bodily life is particularly difficult when observing its death. Wallace suggests that "it takes a lot of intellectual gymnastics and behaviorist hairsplitting not to see struggling, thrashing, and lid-clattering" (248–49) as just the kind of behavior toward pain that would be expressive of a preference on the lobster's part not to be undergoing the experience to which it has been subjected. He ends his article by asking the read-

---

with human conduct if a fish, shrimp, comb jelly, or bird is to seem real to us—as real a living creature as he actually is" (1986, 5).

26. The essay is reprinted in Wallace (2006, 235–54), to which the page numbers in the following discussion refer.

ers of *Gourmet* how they manage their imaginative knowledge of the suffering endured by the animals they eat:

> Do you think much about the (possible) moral status and (probable) suffering of the animals involved? If you do, what ethical convictions have you worked out that permit you not just to eat but to savor and enjoy flesh-based viands . . . If, on the other hand, you'll have no truck with confusions or convictions and regard stuff like the previous paragraph as just so much fatuous navel-gazing, what makes it feel truly okay, inside, to just dismiss the whole thing out of hand? That is, is your refusal to think about any of this the product of actual thought, or is it just that you don't want to think about it? And if the latter, then why not? Do you ever think, even idly, about the possible reasons for your reluctance to think about it? (253–54)

Wallace does not suggest answers to his questions, but it seems clear that the explanation to which he is leaning is some kind of brain balkanization in meat eaters, an ability to ignore, forget, or otherwise disregard the suffering of the animals they eat, even when that suffering is physically present to them. Why should this be so? Is it simply because it is the suffering of animals, not human beings? Adam Smith suggests that the answer may not be so simple. In *The Theory of Moral Sentiments*, he asserts that the experience of having a body of our own is what grounds our imaginative sympathy with the pain of others but also claims that "the little sympathy which we feel with bodily pain is the foundation of the propriety of constancy and patience in enduring it." By way of proof, he points to the Greek tragedies that attempt "to excite compassion by the representation of bodily pain" as being "among the greatest breaches of decorum of which the Greek theatre has set the example" (1.2.1.11–12; Smith 2002, 37).

The physical agonies of Hercules and Hippolytus, Smith argues, "are interesting only because we foresee that death is to be the consequence," whereas "if those heroes were to recover, we should think the representation of their sufferings perfectly ridiculous" (1.2.1.11–12; p. 37). Physical pain is truly interesting to us and excites lasting sympathy only when we can insert it in a narrative and engage in some form of emplotment. The narrative structures that enable compassion in literature must also be operative in everyday experience if sympathetic identification is to be sustained. Why, then, should they fail in the case of an animal whose death we actually witness?

Smith offers an answer in his discussion of condolence. He suggests that "when I condole with you for the loss of your only son, in order to enter into your grief I do not consider what I, a person of such a character and profession, should suffer, if I had a son, and if that son was unfortunately to die; but I consider what I should suffer if I was really you, and I not only change circumstance with you, but I change persons and characters" (7.3.1.4; p. 374). As Smith sees it, sympathy requires experiencing the life of another as if it were one's own, and this in turn requires being able to inhabit another's present suffering as an event within a narrative as it has unfolded up to the moment of suffering. We can now discern an answer to Wallace's questions. It is not that lobster eaters do not imagine the animals experiencing pain—they do so with such ease that lobsters vendors try to convince them that this pain is purely imaginary. It is rather that lobster eaters do not imagine this pain as an event in a life story, even when it ends in death, right before their eyes. The lobster's demise is experienced as merely the cessation of existence, not the conclusion of a narrative into which the observer enters by witnessing it.

To experience an animal's life as a life requires a more sustained effort at understanding than the momentary knowledge of the bat on the wing or the lobster in the pot that emerges from shared corporeality.[27] So let us consider two poems that endeavor to enable such understanding in the case of lobsters. The first is by Carl Rakosi:[28]

THE LOBSTER
to W. Carlos Williams

Eastern Sea, 100 fathoms,
green sand, pebbles,
broken shells.

Off Suno Saki, 60 fathoms,
gray sand, pebbles,
bubbles rising.

27. Cf. Kroodsma on the understanding of the lives of birds that emerges from studying the role their songs play in maintaining social and familial networks: "To look a songbird in the eye is to see him as an individual, one who has grandparents, one who not that long ago was just an egg and songless" (2005, 42).
28. Rakosi 1986, 84–85.

Plasma-bearer
and slow-
motion benthos!

The fishery vessel *Ion*
drops anchor here
                    collecting
plankton smears and fauna.

Plasma-bearer, visible
sea purge,
                sponge and kelpleaf.
Halicystus the Sea Bottle

resembles emeralds
and is the largest
cell in the world.

Young sea horse
Hippocampus twenty
minutes old,

nobody has ever
seen this marine
freak blink.

It radiates on
terminal vertebra
a comb of twenty

upright spines
and curls
its rocky tail.

Saltflush lobster
bull encrusted swims

backwards from the rock.

Rakosi's poem is exacting: it is full of measurements, and Halicystus and Hippocampus are likely to be making their poetic debuts here. It is within their precisely demarcated environment that the poem's narrative—essentially a single action—takes place: "Saltflush lobster | bull encrusted swims | | backwards from the rock." In response to the sea horse curling its rocky tail? We don't know and can't know, but the lobster's movement, in a single stroke, brings the poem's undersea world to life as a place inhabited by sentient beings. It is what gives the poem its title and makes it an exercise of the literary imagination, not merely a list of facts.[29]

Rakosi's poem is dedicated to William Carlos Williams and was originally printed with his response alongside it:[30]

RHYMED ADDRESS: THE LOBSTER
Rhymed address to Carl Rakosi
acknowledging (with thanks)
the excellence of his poem—

The Lobster:

Superb light
and life which in
the mind seems

red even when we know
it must be
green—

luminosity of genius
which strikes
livening it

29. Cf. Naess on the microscopic *Eutreptiella gymnastica*: "I once saw such an organism through my microscope in a little raindrop. It moved around the droplet like a ballet dancer. But the droplet quickly began evaporating. The movements became stiff and less graceful. It made sense to me to save the organism for its own sake by hurrying to fetch more water. I did not believe that the organism had the capacity to suffer. But I believe I might call this identifying with a living creature, even if it was one that was considerably different from myself" (2002, 106).

30. Williams (1986–88, 1.364–65). Details of the original publication with Rakosi's poem in the *Westminster Review* of 1933 can be found at 1.535.

even to the ocean's
bed!
The sun

which makes
leaves of two colors
dark and bright

in every tree
flower tho' he may
lacks light

without that final
brilliance
for me

Williams praises the "luminosity" of Rakosi's genius that, as it strikes the lobster on the dark ocean bed, brings it to life as the living being that it is within its own distinctive habitat. The enlivening force of Rakosi's imagination is more effective than the sun, for while the sun gives leaves their alternating pattern of light and dark, trees, lobsters, and even the sun itself, lack light without the "final brilliance" of the imagination that allows readers of the poem to grasp their interactions as events in a life.

OUTLINE OF THIS BOOK

"The Lobster" is anything but an anomaly in the corpus of William Carlos Williams's poetry. He wrote dozens of poems about animals, including his last, and, in the first chapter, I explore the long poem *Paterson* and the late collections *The Desert Music*, *Journey to Love*, and *Pictures from Breughel* in an effort to disclose the relationship between their intense cathexis to vulnerable, injured, or dying animals, and the formal ambitions Williams claimed for his work at this time.

In *Paterson*, Williams signals an interest in the metrical innovations of the archaic Greek poet Hipponax, and my discussion of *Paterson* is preceded by a study of the two major figures of the Greek iambic tradition, Archilochus and Hipponax. For these poets, as for Williams—the "Diogenes of modern poetry," as Wallace Stevens called him—the insistence that human beings' emotional experience is continuous with that of other animals marks the poet as an outsider with regard to the norms of cultural expression against which this assertion is made. In particular, the articulation of aggression continuous with its expression in nonhuman life singles out its exponent as an unintegrated member of the human society to which he ought to belong even as it connects him with a larger domain of animal affects.

In the second chapter, I turn from aggression as a mode of cathexis to other animals to human aggression directed at them. I begin with Gustave Flaubert's hunting story, "La légende de saint Julien L'Hospitalier," which I read as a critique of the anti-organicism of Symbolist aesthetics, and I investigate the origins of Symbolism's aversion to nonhuman life in the narcissism of Milton's Satan. Arguing that satanic narcissism offers a deep myth with which to understand human beings' destructive aggression toward other animals, I look at alternatives to the human fixation upon self-image in the sonnets of Gerard Manley Hopkins and the late *Cantos* of Ezra Pound. I conclude the chapter with an effort to theorize their poetry as the movement from *historia*, first person exploration of other beings, to *poiesis*, the reflective elaboration that follows upon it, as Martin Heidegger conceives this movement in his discussions of lyric poetry.

In the second part of the book, I look at two different kinds of attempt to imagine the removal of the boundary separating human beings from other animals. I begin the third chapter with a discussion of the correlation between articulate utterance and social complexity in Aristotle's zoological and political works, which leaves open the possibility that birds may be capable of a degree of political organization comparable to that of human beings. I then contrast Aristotle's curiosity about the social lives of other animals with Aristophanes' *Birds*, Herman Melville's *Moby-Dick*, and Louis-Ferdinand Céline's *Rigadoon*, in all of which isolated individuals who have fallen out of human society experience some form of fascination with the social groups of animals they discover beyond its confines.

In the narratives of Aristophanes, Melville, and Céline, human fascination with the sociality of other animals is ultimately thwarted: the protagonists either recreate the human society they had wished to leave or are abandoned by the animal society they had wished to join. In the fourth chapter, I consider narratives in which being or becoming something other than a human being is possible, because the human body is imagined either already to contain the nonhuman or to be capable of transformation into it. I begin with an iambic poem by Semonides that contrasts the nature of women, who participate in a broad spectrum of nonhuman life, with the unmediated humanity of men, who do not. I then discuss a number of episodes from Ovid's *Metamorpho-*

ses that describe becoming an animal, and I conclude with a reading of H. P. Lovecraft's "The Shadow Over Innsmouth," a story whose engagement with the traditions of metamorphosis narrative proceeds from an understanding of the emergence of human from nonhuman life in evolutionary theory.

The movement of the second half of the book mirrors that of its first half. As aggression is disempowered and made abject for the single human animal, but empowered as collective expression, so the fantasy of belonging to a nonhuman collective is denied, but the possibility of individual metamorphosis enabled. Consideration of the desires that animate these fantasies and frustrations will have led me to the erasure of the difference between human being and animal, and between artifact and nature, currently contemplated by posthumanist theory in its engagement with the biological sciences. Wanting to linger a while on the threshold of this posthuman, postanimal world, I end the book with a discussion of Bill Viola's video work *I Do Not Know What It Is I Am Like*, which, I argue, provides an ideal opportunity both to look back over the modes of engagement with other animals explored in the preceding chapters and to reflect more generally on the imaginative engagement with what is other than ourselves that has shaped the pre-posthuman world we are about to leave behind.

PART ONE

The Abject Animal

CHAPTER ONE

The Beast in Pain

Abjection and Aggression in Archilochus and
William Carlos Williams

When charmed by the beauty of that viper, did it never occur to you to change personalities with him? to feel what it was to be a snake? to glide unsuspected in grass? to sting, to kill at a touch; your whole beautiful body one iridescent scabbard of death? —Herman Melville, *The Confidence-Man*

In this chapter I want to look at assertions of emotional continuity between human beings and other animals, particularly in the areas of aggression and wounding, as they appear in the poetry of William Carlos Williams and the Greek iambic poets whose work he saw as analogous to his own. In order to do so, I want to begin in a place that may seem surprising, namely, Wordsworth's preface to the *Lyrical Ballads* and the relationship between emotion and poetic expression that is articulated there. For Wordsworth's familiar claim about the nature of poetry—that it is "the spontaneous overflow of powerful feelings"—requires psychic chemistry whose formulas are helpful in understanding the states of abjection from which the poetry of Williams and his Greek predecessors emerges.

In order to write poetry, Wordsworth argues, a poet must gather inert emotion in his tranquil soul, where it is to be contemplated by him, "till, by a species of reaction, the tranquility gradually disappears, and an emotion, kindred to that which was before the subject of contemplation, is gradually produced." Once this emotion exists in the poet's mind, composition can begin, and it is in the mood created by the revivification of past feeling that his work is carried to its end. Wordsworth thinks this is an enjoyable process and that the poet must take care to communicate to his reader the pleasure he takes in his passions along with the passions themselves, whatever those passions happen to be. The poet requires only a reader whose mind is "sound and vigorous" in order to communicate to him the same pleasure in his feelings as he himself has taken.[1]

The poet, then, as Wordsworth imagines him, has the power to arrest his affective metabolism and to reenergize feelings that would otherwise pass out of his being by dwelling upon them. Indeed, bringing dormant emotion back to life is the psychic labor his work entails, and transmission of this emotion to others is the end he means his work to achieve. The caveat in the formulation is the hope that the reader will be strong enough to handle what the poet has given him to experience. For Wordsworth discusses neither the kinds of emotion that go into poetry beyond his assertion that they must all be made enjoyable nor the long term effects upon the poet of treating his soul as a kind of crucible in which dead feeling is brought back to life by contemplation.

In the case of the ancient poetry of aggression, we do have a brief indication of the psychic consequences of the labor it entails from the perspective of Pindar, who, in his second *Pythian Ode*, distances his own work from it:

εἶδον γὰρ ἑκὰς ἐὼν τὰ πόλλ᾽ ἐν ἀμαχανίᾳ
ψογερὸν Ἀρχίλοχον βαρυλόγοις ἔχθεσιν
πιαινόμενον.

[I have looked from a distance at Archilochus the abuser fattening himself on heavy worded hatreds, and helpless for the most part.] (*P.* 2.54–56)[2]

Archilochus, as Pindar sees him, has bloated himself with his hatred: "fattening" (πιαινόμενον) is a word used in animal husbandry that suggests the unnatural swelling of an animal's body and the lengthy procedures required to induce it.[3] However, while the fattening of an animal equips it for the service it is to perform, Archilochus's force-feeding of himself results in a state of incapacity or helplessness (ἀμαχανία), the opposite of the ability or power

1. Wordsworth 1904, 740.

2. All translations throughout the book are my own.

3. Aristotle *History of Animals* 603b27, on fattening pigs; Euripides *Cyclops* 333, on herd animals. Recent discussions of the poem have connected the word with aristocratic critiques of gluttony: see Steiner (2002, 300–2), Brown (2006, 36–46), and the fundamental discussion of Nagy (1979, 224–26) to which they refer.

(μαχανά), Pindar elsewhere claims for his own work.[4] Finally, Pindar presents himself as a wary spectator of Archilochus's misery, as if his aggressive display were too dangerous, or too disgusting, to approach.

Other ancient authors also point to a link between aggression and exhibitionism in Archilochus. Dio Chrysostom claims that, in his hostility to others, the poet "first of all abuses himself" (*Orations* 33.11–12), Origen that he used his poetic gifts to put on show a character that is licentious and impure (*Against Celsus* 3.25), and Plutarch that, in the unseemly and unrestrained things he says about women, he makes a spectacle, or an example, of himself (*On Curiosity* 10.520a-b). The lengthiest treatment of the topic is found in Aelian, who tells us that Critias, the sophist and relative of Plato, blamed the poet because he "spoke very badly of himself," listing all the shameful things we would not know about him if he had not told us himself. By showing us why he became an object of hatred to those around him, Archilochus, Critias concludes, "was not a good witness on his own behalf" (*Historical Miscellanies* 10.12).

It is easy enough to connect Critias's position with Pindar's as implied praise of aristocratic reserve. What is more difficult to understand is why such unrestrained self-expression is claimed to be a form of incapacity. In the same poem in which he refers to Archilochus, Pindar connects his own work—praise—with the work of the judges of the underworld who, like him, have to formulate and articulate correct judgments about the human beings it is their task to consider. Pindar calls the fruit of Rhadamanthys' mind "blameless" or "blame-free" (ἀμώμετον); while passing judgment may mean condemning, it does not entail the psychic conditions involved in blameful aggression, and Rhadamanthys does not "delight his spirit with the falsehoods that please the minds of slanderers" (*P.* 2.73–75).

Approval and condemnation, as Pindar sees them, are complementary; they map onto praise and criticism—the speech acts in which these verdicts may be elaborated at greater length—but they belong to a different area of psychic life than flattery and abuse, which only seem to resemble them. The latter are insubstantial and ineffective forms of positivity and negativity that cannot disclose anything real about their objects because they originate in affective states not judgments. The speech of abusers is imagined as the outcome and manifestation of a trauma: in attempting to measure other men, and even the gods, by their own standards, they "pierce their own hearts with a

4. Miller 1981, 139–41.

painful wound before they attain what they have cunningly devised in their minds" (*P.* 2.91–92). In an ideal community their speech carries no conviction because its members understand that it is born of feeling not judgment. Even if abusers have the spirit of a fox, they get nothing from their cunning; they are an incapable, self-defeating evil no one bothers to contend with—an ἄμαχον κακόν—and they can accomplish nothing for themselves (2.73–78).[5]

As Pindar sees it, one consequence of narcissistic wounds—the interruption of solipsistic grandiosity by sounder judgment—is an affective state that renders the victim incapable of responding to them effectively. Abusive speech merely displays the wound its speaker cannot acknowledge as such, and is incapable of producing conviction in the speaker or his audience. Because the abuser's speech is ineffective, it is endless, and he distends himself with hatred he cannot discharge. This is the structure of abjection, a negative version of responsibility in which the self is constantly alive to the claims of others but can only respond to them with aggressive denials.

For ancient critics of his poetry, Archilochus is claimed by his own wounded response to others to the extent that he loses control over his own powers of signification and makes himself into a spectacle instead. He is therefore rightly compared to an animal that manifests its feelings in bodily display without self-regulation.[6] Archilochus himself, as one might expect, has a rather different understanding of the relationship between animality and self-expression that appears in his work. In a well-known fragment, he contrasts the cunning of the fox that "knows many tricks," with the single-minded behavior of the hedgehog that knows "one big one" (frag. 201 West), and, in other poems, he identifies himself with both sides of this contrast. He echoes the defensive aggression of the hedgehog in an assertion of his own power to wound—"I know one big thing, how to repay one who has harmed me

5. Cf. J. M. Bell 1984, 14–18.

6. Compare Lévinas (1981, 72–80) on the "traumatic hold" of being for another manifested by Odysseus's dog Argus upon his master's return and why such displays fall short of human sincerity because they are unable to point to their own condition of exposure, remaining trapped in the mere act of being exposed instead (143). Lévinas goes some way toward transvaluing the notorious shamelessness of dogs in Greek culture, on which see Redfield (1994, 193–202) and Steiner (2001). But as Derrida (1992, 86–87) has remarked, the supposed inability of nonhuman animals to hide their feelings remains a *topos* in philosophical accounts of human exceptionalism; cf. Lippit (2000, 30), and Heath (2005, 73–77), on the importance of self-control in Greek speech. The contrast between self-display and critical judgment is conflated by Horace in his account of his satirical predecessor Lucilius, whose work reveals its poet "lying open to view, as if depicted on a votive tablet" (*Satires* 2.1.33), but which was, he claims, welcomed by contemporaries as a sincere effort to correct their vices (2.1.64–65).

with astounding pains" (frag. 126 West)—and, in an extended animal fable, he identifies his own cunning with that of the fox.

The animal fable in which this identification appears dramatizes Archilochus's relations with Lycambes, a person who had promised his daughter to the poet in marriage but later reneged on their agreement (frag. 172–81 West). In the Aesopic version of the fable (1 Perry), a fox and an eagle become friends, thinking that their association will be of mutual benefit. One day when the fox is out hunting, however, the eagle steals its cubs and feeds them to its young. Since the eagle's nest is beyond its reach, the fox is unable to take revenge immediately, but curses the eagle instead, and this curse proves effective: meat the eagle takes from a sacrificial altar sets its nest on fire, and its unfledged offspring fall to the ground, where the fox eats what is left of them.

The fragments of Archilochus's version tell a story of victimization, powerlessness, and hate. The eagle scorns the fox; from his vantage point of lofty superiority, he looks on complacently as his erstwhile ally is consumed by his apparently hopeless desire for revenge, and will not deign to engage him in open combat. Archilochus stresses the horror of the eagle's "unlovely feast" and the grief it causes the fox as a parent (frag. 175, 179 West). Unable to find an outlet for his pain in physical aggression, the fox turns to trickery, calling upon Zeus, to whom "the hubris and the justice of both men and animals are a concern" (frag. 177 West), and he is finally able to satisfy his wounded feelings by mocking the eagle for the burns he suffers in the attempt to rescue his children.

The fable is framed by a direct address to Lycambes in which Archilochus inflicts the humiliation of public interrogation upon him, asking why he thought he could get away with cheating him and inviting him to confess that he must have been out of his mind to try it, now that he can see himself as "a complete laughing stock to his fellow citizens" (frag. 172 West). The specular situation has been reversed, just as it was in the fable, with the comfortable, powerful observer now an object of public ridicule. A wounded person has used cunning and abusive speech to enlist a civic body in his triumph—the very scenario Pindar declared impossible—but the trick on which his success depends is not recorded in the fragments of the poem we have. To understand the nature of the vengeance it involved we must turn to the fragments of another poem, in which Archilochus describes the seduction of his intended bride's younger sister (frag. 196a West).

This poem must have begun by setting up the dramatic irony that informs the long fragment of it that we have, for the younger sister evidently does not recognize the poet and tells him that, if he is experiencing an urgent need for scx, shc has a sister at home who is ready and eager for marriage. The poet replies that he can be satisfied with some kind of sexual contact other than inter-course and that he wants this from her, since her sister is "overripe," and the virginal bloom she once had is now gone. In addition, he claims, she is an evil-tempered, deceitful nymphomaniac who would make him a laughing stock to his neighbors if he were to marry her. He is afraid, he says, that if he is too eager in his desire for satisfaction, he will "give birth to blind and untimely offspring like the bitch in the story," and the girl, apparently unfazed by this tirade against her sister, acquiesces to a lesser form of sexual contact: he lays her down among flowers "like a fawn," and, taking hold of her breasts, ejaculates over her body.[7]

The experience of connection to animal life stages the achievement of abject aggression. The predator's grasp of the fawn in the grass needs no comment, but commentators have attempted to emend away the striking image in which Archilochus compares himself to a pregnant dog, arguing that an adult male Greek could not refer to himself giving birth even in a metaphor.[8] Archilochus is not referring literally to the birth of children, however, since he has made it abundantly clear that he has no intention of marrying the older sister, which is the condition for intercourse with her, and is in the process of trying to get something other than this from the younger one. His fear that he may "give birth to blind and untimely offspring" appears at the end of his tirade against the older girl, which is presented as part of a dramatic dialogue with the younger, but before the successful seduction that rather surprisingly follows it, and which is told as retrospective narrative to an external audience. The expression of fear thus seems to be a kind of aside in which Archilochus jok-ingly imagines the possibility that, by abusing the older girl too vehemently within the poem, he may jeopardize the vengeance against her and her family that has taken the form of a deceptive seduction of her younger sister, and which must be an accomplished fact for the poem to be performed in the first place.

Archilochus's suggestion that he is in danger of becoming "a laughing stock to his neighbors" is a frame-breaking nod to the reversal of specularity ven-geance demands. Knowingness is further signaled by a reference to animal fable within the narrative, as the poet compares himself to "the bitch in the story" (ἡ κύων), the one everyone knows about. Self-identification as the protagonist

---

7. The verbal expression with which the poem ends is ἀφῆκα μένος ("I let go my strength"), with an incomplete adjective preserved that most likely agrees with μένος ("strength"). An epi-gram of Dioscorides (*AP* 5.55) refers to the emission of λευκὸν μένος ("white strength") at the climax of lovemaking, and, given that this poet also has a poem about the daughters of Lycambes (*AP* 7.351), most editors have supplemented λευκὸν μένος here and understood a reference to ejaculation (see Van Sickle 1995, 147–48).

8. For discussion of the proposed emendations, see A. P. Burnett (1983, 92–93).

of an animal fable appears as a canceled possibility: the poet will not fail in his purposes like a dog that gives birth to abortive offspring. On the other hand, the image with which this assertion is made enacts the antisocial energies of abuse poetry, which makes a spectacle of what ought not to be made public. Images of animal maternity have an august epic pedigree as expressions of social and familial responsibility.[9] Archilochus deforms them here to express the triumph of abjection's negative version of commitment while at the same time referring to the fable genre he himself employs on other occasions, within which animals are properly narrative subjects and not merely matter for comparison.

Archilochus offers a twofold answer to Pindar's critique of his animality. First, the connection to animal life that emerges from the unrestrained indulgence of his own feelings allows him to formulate precisely observed resemblances between human and animal behavior, particularly in situations of sex and violence, and this is a cognitive capacity his enemies would do well to be mindful of.[10] In addition, the poet readily admits that these displays of aggression are continuous with those of other animals. We have seen the poet as fox, hedgehog, and dog, and he even compares himself on one occasion to an ant, warning a woman of the dire consequences of not granting him her sexual favors:

ἐπ]ίσταμαί τοι τὸν φιλ[έο]ν[τα] μὲν φ[ι]λεῖν,
τὸ]ν δ᾽ ἐχθρὸν ἐχθαίρειν τε [κα]ὶ κακο[
μύ]ρμηξ.

[I know how to love the one who loves me, but also how to hate and harm my enemy as an ant.] (frag. 23.14–16 West)[11]

9. Achilles compares his labors on behalf of the Greek army to that of a hen bringing food to its chicks (*Iliad* 9.323–26), and Homer compares Odysseus in his anger at the suitors to a bitch barking over its puppies (*Odyssey* 20.13–16). The conclusions of Heath (2005, 48–49) about such animal imagery in Homer in many respects confirm the findings of Snell (1982, 201–3); rather than constructing difference, it figures continuities of behavior between humans and other animals. Cf. Levaniouk (1999) on what Penelope has in common with the water bird that is her namesake, and Padel (1992, 148–50) on the limitations of the "boundary" image for understanding the relationship between humans and other animals in tragedy.

10. A woman waves her arms during sex "as a kingfisher flaps on a protruding rock" (frag. 41 West), a man's penis is swollen "like that of a grain-fed breeding ass from Priene" (frag. 43 West), a woman's genitals look like the young of a nightingale (frag. 263 West), a man is given the name "red deer" because of his cowardice (frag. 280 West), another cowers "like a partridge" (frag. 224 West).

11. Cf. frag. 126 West, frag. 201 West, on the hedgehog, and frag. 1 West, a general claim to skill.

The vehemence of the identification is striking. The poet does not claim "I know how to hate and harm like an ant," but, literally, "I, an ant, know how to hate and harm." The animal is in the nominative case and agrees with the subject of the sentence, which it follows emphatically, with the additional force of enjambment. Archilochus does not imagine ant being as the communal industry of the superorganism that, in the Aesopic fable (373 Perry), makes the ant a fitting contrast to the idly singing cicada. The ant is not, as it is for Aristotle, one of the political animals among whom "one activity is common to all" (*History of Animals* 1.1.488a8–13). If this ant ever belonged to a *polis*, he does so no longer, but comes "as a lone ant from a broken ant-hill," like Pound's "ego scriptor" (*Canto* LXXVI, 472).

The isolation of ant being as Archilochus imagines it intensifies the desire, the vulnerability, and the aggression of the animal that they both are. In what follows, he tells the woman she has taken by storm a city that men have never captured, and he invites her to possess it and "rule over it with tyranny" (frag. 23.17–21 West).[12] The poet figures his own desire as victimization by its object and retaliates with a whole body yearning for physical aggression that is, however, imagined as the tiny harm of a single ant bite.[13] His ability to act out his grandiose affective drives on the scale his heart desires is as limited as the power of the animal to injure what is vastly larger than itself. The poet's ant self is as circumscribed as an insect, from a human perspective, is spectacularly constrained by the tiny form it inhabits.[14]

How are we to square this humorous acknowledgment of the abject animal's limitations with the desires that animate the Lycambes story? Archilochus's public shaming of Lycambes' daughters is not likely to strike an impartial observer as a measured response to their father's withdrawal of an offer of marriage to the elder, nor is an indifferent person likely to rejoice in the suicide of the entire family that is envisaged as its outcome.[15] The wounded ego

12. West 1974, 119; A. P. Burnett 1983, 71–76.

13. Cf. Watson (1995), on the blend of victimized feebleness and compensatory aggression in Horace's *Epodes*.

14. Compare the poem in which Archilochus warns someone that he has "a cicada by the wing" (frag. 223 West): the traditional connection between cicadas and poets as singers is coupled with a reference to the defenselessness of an insect that lacks a bite or sting with which to defend itself. As Clay (2004, 24–26) notes, this poem seems to be referred to in stories of the poet's death at the hands of a man named Raven, who is told by Apollo that he can avoid the hatred due to the killer of a poet if he travels to the place "where the Cicada is buried."

15. Cf. Smith (1.3.4.8–1.3.5.4; 2002, 27–30), who argues that the enjoyment of vengeance remains incomplete without sympathetic spectators, but that the recruitment of spectators requires the injured party to moderate his heart's desire for unlimited punishment with con-

seems not so much to lose the ability to rationally assess the scale of its injuries in the experience of its own pain—as when, for example, Medea responds to Jason's desire for a new wife by killing their children—but rather to deliberately jettison any effort to do so, and to revel instead in the pleasure of its powerful feelings.

The extravagance of the response can only remind the wounded ego of the degree to which it has been humbled by its injury. The more catastrophic the satisfaction it seeks, the more it betrays its inferiority to what has injured it, and the more it reinscribes the humiliation vengeance is intended to redress.[16] And yet the poet presses on, assuming that he will carry his audience with him into the territory in which an unlimited desire to wound becomes a feeling of continuity with all the forms of nonhuman aggression he sees in the world around him. To invoke fictionality seems beside the point: Archilochus's poems are not the playful nip of a cat in which bite is mimed without a genuine intention to hurt.[17] The pleasure of unlimited wounding, and of the bottomless vulnerability in which it originates, are the emotions the poet gives us to enjoy, regardless of their practical consequences.

Archilochus embraces resentment's choral demands thematically, in the claim that he has made his enemies objects of public ridicule instead of himself, and formally, in the frame-breaking narration that recruits his audience as firsthand witnesses of the triumphs he narrates. He does so with a complete disregard for the right of others to be represented in a manner to which they would assent, serving up their vulnerability as of a piece with his own.[18]

---

sideration of what would be deemed equitable by such impartial observers, whose sympathies will otherwise be alienated.

16. Cf. Bernstein: "*Ressentiment* is trapped forever in the slights of the past" (1992, 28).

17. Rosen (2007, 243–68) argues that ancient readers hostile to Archilochus, such as Pindar and Critias, failed to appreciate that his poems were fictions. On the nip as not a bite, see Bateson (1972, 177–93), whose cat was perhaps less inclined than some to make overstepping the line between the two part of the game in which it occurs. For a suggestion that Archilochus's poetry was intended to reinforce normative values by dramatizing their opposite, see Bartol (1993, 74–75) and Brown (1997, 16–25, 41–42).

18. On the right to self-representation in life writing, and its impingement upon the rights of others to fair portrayal, see Eakin (1992, 50–53), Couser (2004, x–xii, 18–30), and Mills (2004, 111–18). Kantian notions of respect for autonomous persons and the avoidance of deliberate harm loom large in these discussions of authorial responsibility, and they mesh easily with accounts of fictional value in the main stream of ethical criticism, where it is argued that fictional representations can or should offer readers an account of engagement with others that has a completeness and transparency impossible in real life and so provide them with an image of what ethical behavior ought to be but seldom is; see, for example, Booth (2001) and Nussbaum (1990, 148 67). These claims have been subject to cogent criticism by Charles Altieri in

Archilochus's abjection, like Lear's rage or Swann's jealousy, offers us access to an ecstatic state whose appeal is not easily grasped by mimetic accounts of literary value. Our sympathetic identification with the poet does not help us understand real-world counterparts of his life by giving us access to a transparent imitation of their behavior. Rather, such identification is, when it peaks, a genuinely transcendental experience in which we emerge not just from the affective limitations to which any single human being is inevitably subject, but from humanness altogether. It enables powerful feelings of continuity with the suffering and aggression of nonhuman life as this life expresses itself in the face of human beings and the social forms in which they have regulated their own affective existence.

DEFORMATION AND DEFORMITY

Archilochus's most celebrated successor in the poetry of abjection was Hipponax. Fewer fragments of his poems have survived, and they are less complete than those of Archilochus, so it is difficult to form a satisfactory idea of his achievement. He does seem to be interested in continuities between human and animal behavior, but less as a way of expressing his own affective cravings than as an element in the depiction of scenes of depravity: a man on the toilet squawks like an owl (frag. 61 West), a woman's genitals look like a sea urchin (frag. 70 West), a man on all fours vomits like a dog (frag. 115 West), a greedy man's mouth is as relentless as a heron's beak (frag. 118b West). Ingestion, voiding, and physical abuse are what interest him most, and when animals appear, it is to portray the degradation of a human being reduced to their level through physical constraints.

The most extensive narrative by Hipponax that we have tells of a man tied up by a foreign sex worker, who, unable to communicate his wish that she stop flogging his genitals, soils himself in an excess of pain, at which point he is attacked by a horde of dung beetles attracted by the smell (frag. 92 West).[19] This narrative looks to be thematically continuous with what seems to have been Hipponax's most characteristic representation of the human

---

a series of books and papers that endeavor to show the ways in which the pleasures of powerful feeling are a value in the lives of particular individuals that any ethics of inter-subjective relations should take into account when calculating what is owed to others and ourselves (Altieri 2001, 32; 2003, 22–29, 89).

19. "His sexual adventures, besides being more sordid than any others in ancient literature, have at the same time a farcical element in them . . . They are presented as one ingredient in a picaresque life full of brawling, burglary, poverty and cheap drink" (West 1974, 29).

animal, the figure of the scapegoat, which seems to have occupied a central place in his work. While the impression of centrality may be skewed by an extended sequence of citations on this topic in the Byzantine commentator John Tzetzes, these fragments offer a picture of human degradation by analogy with a vilified nonhuman animal that goes far beyond such portrayals of humiliation in Archilochus.

Tzetzes speaks of the scapegoat as an ancient form of purification in which the ugliest man in a city was selected, had food placed in his hands, and was flogged on his penis with a variety of plants. He was then burned on wood from wild trees and his ashes scattered to the winds and waves (*Chilads* 5.728). He claims that Hipponax describes the practice best, citing lines about being struck with fig branches, about the food the scapegoat is given to eat, and the beating of the genitals (frag. 5–10 West). While we do not know whether the poet is referring to himself or someone else in these lines, they can easily be connected with legends of his ugliness, the portrayal of which is supposed to have initiated quarrels with the sculptors Bupalus and Athenis,[20] with the fragments of the brothel narrative (frag. 92 West), the theme of hunger and deprivation in his self-portrayal (frag. 32–39 West), and what might have been an autobiography in the form of a parody of the life of Odysseus (frag. 128 West), who even in the *Odyssey* has traits of the scapegoat about him.[21]

Hipponax was celebrated in antiquity for a formal innovation in the iambic meter. The basic unit used by Archilochus is ˘ - ˘ -, where ˘ represents a short syllable and - a long one. This basic unit is repeated to produce lines of various lengths. In the first position in the unit, a long syllable may be substituted for a short one, diagrammed x - ˘ -, where x represents this possibility for substitution, and the unit's integrity and discernibility as an iambic shape are guaranteed by the third position, where the short syllable may not be replaced. Hipponax's innovation was to allow substitution in the third position in a unit ending a line, so that lines built out of multiples of the basic unit end not with a clear and distinct impression of its basic iambic building block, but with a jumble of syllables that deform and obscure it. The line's fundamental metrical shape gives out just when it should assert itself most forcefully, and this version of the iambic meter was called "lame," "halting" (χωλός), or "limp," "damaged" (σκάζων).[22]

20. See West (1971, 1:109–10) for the ancient testimony.
21. Especially when on returning to the palace of Aeolus, he is driven away as "the most wretched of living creatures . . . hated by the blessed gods" (*Odyssey* 10.72–75).
22. See Liddell and Scott's *Greek-English Lexicon*, sv, and the detailed description in West, who observes: "This rough treatment of the cadence, normally the most strictly regulated

The regular iambic meter was not exclusively associated with a particular kind of content. While it was typical for first-person expression that involved invective and sexually explicit content, Archilochus uses it for other kinds of material too, and also, conversely, employs elegy for an exhortation to drunkenness (frag. 4 West), and a famous confession of cowardice (frag. 5 West).[23] Hipponax's innovation thus introduced a deformity or deformation into the meter that is itself an index of the abject life whose pleasures his poems record. The choliambic meter is a formal instantiation of the poet's incapacity to master and shape into art the material of his own life that ought to have been plastic in his hands.

For ancient theorists, meter conveys anthropological information. Demetrius, in *On Style* 5, asserts that the hexameter is called heroic because, as a long line, its bulk is appropriate to heroes, whose lives would not be properly instantiated in the brief lines of Archilochus. The iambic meter, by contrast, he claims, is unprepossessing and like ordinary speech, echoing Aristotle's account of it as "the very diction of the mass."[24] Demetrius's anthropology of style is organized according to character types: the grand or aristocratic, the smooth or elegant, the plain or humble, and the forceful or impressive, along with unpleasantly exaggerated versions of themselves they may become—the frigid, the affected, the arid, and the graceless. Meter appears in this account as a formalization of natural language that operates in conjunction with other features of literary discourse to represent styles of human character.

It is regrettable that Demetrius gives himself only four categories to work with, for he includes Hipponax's metrical innovation in his account of the forceful or impressive style by recuperating it as a sign of aggression, instead of attending to the formlessness and incapacity signaled by the name itself: "Wanting to abuse his enemies, [Hipponax] broke up the [iambic] meter, and made it lame instead of straightforward, and unrhythmic, this being appropriate to forcefulness and abusiveness" (301). Demetrius clearly understands that the choliambic line is broken and impeded, and it is hard to see how it can be vigorous and impressive at the same time.

---

part of any verse, may best be understood as a kind of deliberate metrical ribaldry, in keeping with these iambographers' studied vulgarity" (1982, 41). The plural refers to Ananius, a near contemporary of Hipponax, who is credited by some ancient authorities with the invention instead.

23. West 1974, 22–25; Parker 1997, 27–35.

24. *Rhetoric* 1408b33; cf. *Poetics* 1449a24, where it is said that the iambic meter has the rhythm of speech, and that iambic trimeters are produced naturally in ordinary conversation, whereas hexameters only rarely so and in deliberate departures from ordinary language.

In contrast to Demetrius, it seems more productive to suggest that, if Archilochus is concerned with both aggression and humiliation as aspects of abjection, Hipponax is particularly concerned to invent a meter expressive of the latter. Schiller's account of the interaction between sense drive and form drive is helpful in understanding the interaction between experience and its shaping instantiated in Hipponax's choliamb. For Schiller, the sense drive is the psychic faculty that registers the impact of the world; the form drive the defensive response to the prospect of total immersion in the world this receptivity raises. The form drive turns experience into selfhood by organizing it into patterns and so evokes the complementary danger that the self may become closed to new experiences by seeing only what it has already known and mastered in retrospective contemplation.[25] By reversing the usual process in which stichic meters become more regular as they approach the end of the line, Hipponax reverses the relationship between content and form this movement expresses: we see a poetic self constantly overwhelmed and undone by experience.

What happens to Hipponax metrically is consistent with the thematic critique of Archilochus's selfhood as an unregulated input-output mechanism in Pindar and Critias, and with Aristotle's disparagement of iambic poetry as a discourse that consists of unreflective particularities of response. A truly free man, Aristotle claims, will only go so far with mockery and abuse, whereas a buffoon is "mastered by the ridiculous and spares neither himself nor others" (*Nicomachean Ethics* 4.8, 1127b34–28b39). For Aristotle, this distinction between kinds of human being is enacted in the history of genres as the emergence of genuine comedy from iambic abuse. The crucial step toward plots that enact general structures of probability and necessity is the abandonment of actual names, for this marks the poet's ability to rise above the details of actuality in order to discern and make available general patterns of human behavior (*Poetics* 4, 1448b33–49b8, 1451b11). The iambic poet is a man who has been mastered by his experience, and failed to give it shape and significance for others. For his critics, such immersion in the world is rightly described as animal.

25. On the interaction of form drive and sense drive, see Schiller (1967, 11.6–14.1, pp. 74–94), and the helpful discussion in Hammermeister (2002, 51–54).

DESCENDING TO A DOG

Hipponax's poems have a distinctive kinetic feel: the body is present in them in a way that makes the nature of the experience they record palpable and obvious.[26] His achievement, as it is described in John Addington Symonds's *Studies of the Greek Poets*, caught the imagination of William Carlos Williams, who cites this description as a kind of epilogue to Book 1 of *Paterson*:

> In order apparently to bring the meter still more within the sphere of prose and common speech Hipponax ended his iambics with a spondee or a trochee instead of an iambus, doing thus the utmost violence to the rhythmical structure. These deformed and mutilated verses were called χωλίαμβοι or ἴαμβοι σχάζοντες (lame or limping iambics). They communicated a curious crustiness to the style. The choliambi are in poetry what the dwarf or cripple is in human nature. Here again, by their acceptance of this halting meter, the Greeks displayed their acute aesthetic sense of propriety, recognizing the harmony which subsists between crabbed verses and the distorted subjects with which they dealt—the vices and perversions of humanity—as well as their agreement with the snarling spirit of the satirist. Deformed verse was suited to deformed morality.[27]

Symonds distinguishes the Greek iambic poets from the Roman and later European satirists they resemble in certain respects on the basis that they present themselves as an example of the misery they see in others: "A more unhappy existence, wretched in itself and the cause of wretchedness to others, can scarcely be imagined, if the tale of the life of Archilochus be true."[28] It has been suggested that Williams's reference to Hipponax is ironic, a parody of Eliot's footnoting of the tradition.[29] What Williams got from Symonds's

---

26. Cf. Bateson (1972, 178) on "kinesics" as the "involuntary moods signs" of animals that appear in their movements, and the discussion in Wolfe (2003a, 39–40).

27. Symonds 1880, 1.284, cited in Williams 1992, 40.

28. Symonds 1880, 1.278.

29. See Cushman, who makes the mistake made by so many commentators of equating long with epic, and so argues that Williams's intention was to "fashion out of modern American life and speech a poem worthy of inclusion in an epic tradition" (1985, 101). It is regrettable that Cushman did not consider the source of Williams's citation in Symonds more fully, for Symonds describes the emergence of Greek iambic poetry as a countertradition to epic in such a way that the analogies with Williams's understanding of his own relationship to Eliot are

account of the Greek iambic tradition, however, is germane to the project of *Paterson*, and thinking about the relationship between Williams and Hippo-nax is helpful in understanding Williams's generic ambition to create a long poem that is not an epic, but instead a poem about everyday life in which the anger and humiliation of his own involvement in it are central themes.

The structure of *Paterson* is a movement of descent. The poem follows the Passaic River from the falls above Paterson, New Jersey, through the city, to its outlet in Newark Bay near New York City. Descent is thematized in one of its most famous passages—"The descent beckons | as the ascent beckoned"—a passage of sufficient importance to Williams that he published it as an independent poem in *The Desert Music*, and one of the tasks the poem sets itself is to discover how the series of degradations, humiliations, and pol-lutions that the river and its genius, Dr. Paterson, suffer might be understood as a kind of victory: "No defeat is made up entirely of defeat."[30]

The preface that sets out the poem's project is spoken by a dog (3):

> To make a start,
> out of particulars
> and make them general, rolling
> up the sum, by defective means—
> Sniffing the trees,
> just another dog
> among a lot of dogs. What
> else is there? And to do?
> The rest have run out—
> after the rabbits.
> Only the lame stands—on
> three legs. Scratch front and back.
> Deceive and eat. Dig
> a musty bone

This canine seems to be something of a Cynic, as he sniffs the trees in a very public acknowledgment of the bodily functions human beings prefer to con-ceal. But, in his ordinary isolation from his fellows, he is neither a lone wolf

---

clear. Cushman's account of Williams's understanding of meter is unaccountably patronizing. Williams, for example, is quite correct to assert that, for Aristotle, "a certain kind of verse is 'suited to' a certain kind of subject matter" (102), and it is Cushman who is wrong to claim that the relationship between the two was thought by Aristotle to be purely conventional (98–99).

30. Williams (1992, 78–79). All references to *Paterson* are to this edition.

nor a pack dog, or, but "just another dog | among a lot of dogs." Confined by incapacity to the local scene, he is a source of home truths: a dog like this one "blows the gaff," in William Empson's phrase, on cultural pretensions, which are to him mere spoors of self-assertion, to be obliterated by the never-ending stream of newcomers.[31]

Our first taste of the "musty bone" of local knowledge is the Passaic River, which the dog poet tracks from the falls of Paterson into the diversions and dispersions in which its first strong presence is lost. And so we learn that the first task of local poetry is to keep an ear out for a sound stream that was never heard aright by European colonists. Unlike the robin that speaks "Clearly! | clearly!" the River is hard to hear and harder still to put into words: it has as yet "no speech . . . no language" (20).

"Must you taste everything? Must you know everything? | Must you have a part in everything?" Williams asks his nose in the early poem "Smell!"[32] In this section of *Paterson*, the unabashed inquisitiveness of the dog poet's nose morphs into the expansive desire to be one with the River's inhabitants so that he might hear what they hear. For even a snail hears better than the poet; "hedged in by the pouring torrent," it knows the voice of "Earth, the chatterer, father of all | speech" (38–39), and its intimacy with the River is what the dog poet's knowledge of the local wants to become.

The dog poet of Book 2 is more reflective about the other animals he noses out. He stirs up some grasshoppers in Paterson's public park and they remind him of a sculpted grasshopper from Chapultepec, a "matt stone solicitously instructed | to bear away some rumor | of the living presence that has preceded | it." The union of nature and art is perfect: the sculpture's stone wings do not need to unfold for flight because the crafting of the insect at rest is so well attuned to the living animal that "the mind's wings" can do its flying for it. The imaginative union of animal and artist is conceived as the conflu-

31. See Empson (1989, 158–69). If we chart the pedigree of Williams's dog, we can see that he is out of the unabashed satirical dog of the Elizabethans, by the dog that, because it does not hide the truth about itself, is a repository of "the impulses that keep us sane," with some admixture of the unreasoning, faithful dog of modern sentiment. The dogs that have gone off in pursuit of better things have often been thought to be Pound and Eliot, from the reference to *Four Quartets* in the following lines—"For the beginning is assuredly | the end—since we know nothing, pure | and simple, beyond our own complexities." See LeClair (1970, 99), Callan (1992, 183), and Bremen (1993, 180), and cf. Mikkelsen (2003) on Williams's rejection of Eliot's supposed "impersonality" in the context of traditions of self-disclosure in American pragmatism.

32. Williams 1986–88, 1:92. All references to poems other than *Paterson* here and elsewhere are to his two-volume *Collected Poems*.

ence of a receptivity to shaping in the grasshopper itself with the desire for intelligent delineation on the part of the sculptor. Their happy marriage is the opposite of the "divorce" between mind and world that plagues Paterson (and *Paterson*), and the potency of mutual attraction on which it depends is expressed in an image of magical impossibility: "Love that is a stone endlessly in flight" (47–49).[33]

As an image of beauty attained, the grasshopper is past perfect and exotic, and so, predictably enough perhaps, contrasts unfavorably with the poet's failure to articulate the local scene that "the dogs and trees | conspire to invent." His incapacity becomes the abjection of Paterson itself, the "thwarting" and "avulsion" of fecundity seen in its uprooted flowers, dismembered trees, and "men steadfastly refusing" (82). In his despair, however, the hangdog poet is granted a vision of the spirit of the place (83):

> As there appears a dwarf, hideously deformed—
> he sees squirming roots trampled
> under the foliage of his mind by the holiday
> crowds as by the feet of the straining
> minister. From his eyes sparrows start and
> sing. His ears are toadstools, his fingers have
> begun to sprout leaves (his voice is drowned
> under the falls)   .

What the poet sees seems to be a hallucinatory version of Peter the Dwarf, the famous freak of old Paterson whose head and body, buried in separate coffins, were disinterred for investigation in 1885, as described elsewhere in the poem (10, 192). His reconfiguration here is a wildly literal instantiation of Williams's belief in the unifying power of the imagination,[34] and a kind of personification of the saving power of degradation. He brings the poetics of choliambic deformity to life as the fecundity of one who, like the snail,

33. Crickets, grasshoppers, and cicadas have persistent associations with sexual and artistic possibility in Williams's work. In an early poem, "Great Mullen," the poet is to his beloved as an insect is to the plant it would scale, an image of abject desire worthy of Archilochus: "I am a cricket waving his antennae | and you are high, grey and straight. Ha!" (1:163). In another, "Sub Terra," the emergence of seven year cicadas, "thrusting up through the grass, | up under the weeds | answering me" (1:63) figures the emergence of responsive contact with the natural world that is developed more fully in the grasshopper of *Paterson*.

34. See Williams's *Spring and All* on "the unity of understanding which the imagination gives" (1:206), and cf. Markos (1994, 50–55, 115–52), and Bremen (1993, 18–20), on the evolution of Williams's understanding of its unifying power.

lives on intimate terms with the River, and his message to the poet is a brief admonition that resembles a Muse's instruction: "Poet, poet! sing your song, quickly!"

It is as dog poet that Williams is entrusted with the privileged communication from the nonhuman that his task requires, and we are right to feel dismayed that Peter's urgent call for song is followed by the letters from an angry Marcia Nardi to an all too human writer that occupy the end of Book 2. Like the River, the poem is accumulating material that threatens to choke its progress and appears to be in danger of vanishing altogether in the widening pools of local affiliation in which its impetus is spent.[35] Poet and poem lose their direction in quibbles "as to which is the man and | which the thing and of them both which | is the more to be valued" (116). The contortions of syntax mime the river's involution in flood plain and swamp. The aggressive, curious, canine energy that had driven the poem forward has dispersed, and this dissolution of conative, individualizing power is figured as a flood that obliterates form, covering everything with mud so that the true outlines of things are indiscernible (140):

> —fertile (?) mud.

> If it were only fertile. Rather a sort of muck, a detritus,
> in this case—a pustular scum, a decay, a choking
> lifelessness—that leaves the soil clogged after it,
> that glues the sandy bottom and blackens stones—so that
> they have to be scoured three times when, because of
> an attractive brokenness, we take them up for garden uses.
> An acrid, a revolting stench comes out of them, almost one
> might say a granular stench—fouls the mind   .

This is the mud of the inanimate, matter inimical to all forms of life and resistant to both human and canine enlivenment. It invites us to identify the living body with its material components, an imaginative possibility that, as we shall see, Williams would not entertain until his final poems. In *Paterson*, the distinction between animate and inanimate nature remains fundamental, and the conflation of the two signals the same foreclosure of the poet's task

---

35. On *Paterson*'s poetics of inclusion, and the threat to the poem's integrity it poses, see Breslin (1970, 170–72), Lowell (1972, 158–61), Tapscott (1984, 207–23).

as the quote from George Barker that pronounces *Paterson* dead on arrival: "American poetry . . . does not exist" (140). In an incoherent and virtually incomprehensible passage, Williams proposes turning the poem over to "the woman" (Marcia Nardi as Everywoman?), to begin again "with insects | and decay, decay and then insects" (140–41). The poet begs out of his project by making the animals that are frequent figures of the mind's regenerative contact with the world in his work senseless participants in an entropic process, no more receptive to poetic intelligence than mud.

The despair of Book 3 seems not so much to be answered as simply ignored by Book 4, which appears to open on an entirely different work, a dramatic "Idyl" set on Manhattan's Upper East Side. The manifestly artificial and generic quality of the pastoral, in which a rich woman looks out from her apartment window onto the rocks in the water she calls her "sheep" contrasts with the naturalism of the lyrics in which sympathetic identification with the nonhuman is expressed in the earlier books. The woman's indifference to the remnant landscape of which she is the steward—"all that's left of the elemental, the primitive | in this environment" (152)—is a consequence of her vertical separation from the River that the residents of Paterson still live alongside: their degradation is less damaging to the progress of poetry than the Manhattanite's elevation.[36]

From Manhattan, the Atlantic Ocean that "sucks in all rivers" (199), makes itself heard. Its steady roar is "as of a distant waterfall" (202): all that remains of the poet's task is the tiny possibility this "as of" leaves open, namely, that the voice of the waterfall might in some sense be non-identical with the inanimate utterance of the sea. All the poet can do is begin again. He extricates himself from the stream as it is about to merge with the ocean, no longer a dog poet, but a poet accompanied by a dog, and the two of them set off inland to start the journey over.

Williams saw the problem with giving a conclusive finish to a poem that

36. On the central place of remnant landscapes—the cemeteries, hospital grounds, railway embankments, and quarries in which wild nature is able to reassert itself—in Williams's lyrics, see Buell (2001, 84–128). "Tree and Sky" (1:385), "A Bastard Piece" (1:454), "Morning" (1:459), "Franklin Square," (2:124), "To A Lovely Old Bitch" (2:131), and "Song" (2:198) are all excellent examples of his abiding fascination with such spots, and it is rewarding to read them alongside Aldo Leopold's "Prairie Birthday," which celebrates the power of such places to evoke the broken whole of which they are fragments: "Many of these railroad fences were erected before the prairie had been plowed. Within these linear reservations, oblivious of cinders, soot, and annual clean-up fires, the prairie flora still splashes its calendar of colors, from pink shooting-star in May to blue aster in October" (1949, 48).

explores the vagaries of the human subject's dependence on its everyday geo-physical environment.[37] However, he also came to believe that the Odyssean ending he had fashioned for Book 4—the strong suggestion that the journey that has just ended is about be taken up again—inadequately represented his intentions for *Paterson*, and he canceled the implied continuation with the publication of a fifth book that took the poem in an entirely new direction:[38]

> I have come to understand not only that many things have occurred in me and the world, but I have been forced to recognize that there can be no end to such a story I have envisioned with the terms which I had laid down for myself. I had to take the world of Paterson into a new dimen-sion if I wanted to give it imaginative validity. (xv)

Williams's phrasing of what has happened between Books 4 and 5 is strik-ing: he speaks of "things" that have occurred "in" him, not "to" him, mak-ing himself grammatically parallel to "the world" whose imaginative validity he has to reconsider in the light of the things that have taken place in it. The expression seems to point to the debilitating strokes that Williams suffered in the early 1950s, and which reoriented the poetic ambitions of Book 5 (227):

> Paterson has grown older
>
>   the dog of his thoughts
> has shrunk
> to no more than "a passionate letter"
> to a woman, a woman he had neglected
> to put to bed in the past   .
>   And went on
> living and writing
>   answering
> letters

37. See "A Statement by William Carlos Williams About the Poem Paterson," dated May 31, 1951, and included with the prefatory material to the 1992 edition: "I had to think hard as to how I was going to end the poem. It wouldn't do to have a grand and soul satisfying conclusion because I didn't see any in my subject matter" (xiii–xiv).

38. The work toward a sixth book included as an appendix to the 1992 edition was not pub-lished by Williams in his lifetime, and is too incomplete to allow one to discern what its contri-bution to the evolving shape of the poem might have been.

and tending his flower
garden, cutting his grass and trying
to get the young
                    to foreshorten
their errors in the use of words which
he had found so difficult, the errors
he had made in the use of the
poetic line:

The dog poet is no longer an aggressive inquisitor, but a patient animal that, like Odysseus's Argus, has survived everyone's expectations and now lives mostly in, and off, its memories. When Williams describes the Metropolitan Museum's *Hunt of the Unicorn* tapestries, he looks at the hounds with sympathetic nostalgia as they eviscerate themselves in pursuit of a mythical beast. The tapestry reframes the problem of being in the world, and wanting at the same time to grasp the world with the mind, that leaves the dog poet of Books 1–4 chasing his own tale. For the invention of the unicorn makes imagination itself the object of the quest, not the means by which some truth other than itself is to be captured, and this understanding is inscribed in the tapestry as the ritualized behavior of the hunt that, like dance, transforms the aggressive energy of vigorous young animals into harmonious patterns of species-appropriate behavior.[39]

As Williams sees it now, there is both a phylogenetic and an ontogenetic propriety to the history of the human imagination. Hence he is more indulgent toward the decorum of historical forms of artistic achievement, even as he is in search of the mode of imaginative understanding proper to his own old age.[40] So the bodies of the wounded dogs that lie dead and dying among the tapestry flowers remind the poet of the death of a snake he witnessed as a child, and of the words of a cousin who told him that "its tail | would not stop wriggling till | after the sun | goes down" (229–32), and this confluence of a thematics of unanticipated harm with a poetics of confessional disclosure points to the imaginative undertaking Williams would increasingly deem appropriate to his own later work: images of catastrophic damage to the body

---

39. Cf. the excellent discussion of dance in Book 5 in Breslin (1970, 225–32).

40. Charles Olson deprecated Book 5's celebration of "the achieved artifact" over the display of energy in action in Books 1–4; see the discussion of Olson's comments in relation to his theory of projective verse in Von Hallberg (1974, 36–37).

of another animal, either unfolding slowly from within, or happening suddenly from without, are replayed and interrogated for the light they shed on the relationship between embodiment and poetic achievement.[41]

Williams communicates the strong feelings that emerge from this confluence of thematics and poetics through increasing refinement of the triadic verse that, he believed, had allowed him to eliminate his errors "in the use of the | poetic line." Williams looked to the Greek iambic tradition in *Paterson* not as a model for his own metrical invention but as an analogue to it: Symonds's claim that "the choliambi are in poetry what the dwarf or cripple is in human nature" offered a nice equivalent to the three-footed dog poet Williams felt he had to become for the purposes of the poem. What I want to suggest in the remainder of this chapter is that the biopoetics of Williams's later poetry—the union of a fully mastered verse form capable of registering the particularities of individual animal lives, both human and nonhuman, with the full thematic disclosure of the human being as one animal among others—keeps an ear open for the lameness of Hipponax's choliamb in its efforts to communicate the experience of physical impediment by formal means. Indeed, insofar as the aggression of the dog poet of Books 1–4 of *Paterson* offers one half of a poetry of iambic abjection, the later poetry's disclosure of the vulnerability of the poet's conative drives to unpredictable physical curtailment can be understood as the fulfillment of the iambic project *Paterson*'s epigraph announces.

The Desert Music signals an intention to reconsider the iambic poetics of *Paterson* by reprinting the passage on descent as the first poem in the collection. Its claim that "the descent | made up of despairs | and without accomplishment" can be a kind of awakening (Williams 1986–1988, 2:245) is subject to special interrogation now that the incapacity it celebrates extends to basic functions of sustenance and support. In "For Eleanor and Bill Monahan," the fragility of an elderly couple who have come to so depend on one another that the loss of either one entails the collapse of the other is contrasted with the freedom of migratory birds who "know how | to escape suffering | by flight" (2:253). The sight of these flocking birds enables a momentary flight from individual incapacity into the anonymity of collective endeavor, but mostly Williams is too attentive to the suffering or incapacity of individual animals

41. On the theme of animal suffering in the late poetry, see M. M. Clark, who sees it as "a vivid metaphor for the human being under conditions of suffering" (2004, 231), particularly insofar as human beings in extreme physical pain may lose their recourse to the consolation of language.

to allow himself fantasies of this kind; the pet goose of "To Daphne and Virginia" is as trapped in its body as the poet, its efforts to move as futile as his own attempts to overcome the "stammer" that impedes his family's efforts to communicate with one another (2:246):

> Men
> against their reason
>   speak of love, sometimes,
>   when they are old. It is
> all they can do   .
>   or watch a heavy goose
>   who waddles, slopping
>   noisily in the mud of
>   his pool.

The triadic verse bogs down in the mud with the animal whose life it communicates. If we think back to the young Williams's claim that a poem is "a small (or large) machine made of words" (2:54), this mechanism is now one with the soft machine of the animal body wearing out before our eyes. Williams's "abortive rhythms," as Wallace Stevens called them,[42] have abandoned the early modernist fetishization of the inorganic for a Hipponactean biopoetics of abjection. So too, in "To a Dog Injured in the Street," Williams does not ironize or otherwise obfuscate his sentimental identification with the injured animal (2:255):

> It is myself,
>   not the poor beast lying there,
>   yelping with pain
> that brings me to myself with a start—
>   as at the explosion
>   of a bomb, a bomb that has laid
> all the world waste.

Three psychic movements are registered: the dog's injury is a sudden horror; its suffering is like the poet's own; it is for himself that the poet mourns as he watches it die. Williams knows he can instrumentalize the dog's pain as a way of communicating his own, and this knowledge leads him to reflect on

42. Stevens 1957, 257.

poetic narcosis and poetic responsibility as they are instantiated in John Keats and René Char. Keats's "drowsy numbness," in which what pains the mind is drowned in sensory abundance, is countered by Char's minimalist naturalism in which the beauty of the world is somehow able to stand for the suffering the poet has witnessed (2:256):

> I think
> of the poetry
>   of René Char
>   and all he must have seen
> and suffered
>   that has brought him
>   to speak only of
> sedgy rivers,
>   of daffodils and tulips
>   whose roots they water,
> even to the free-flowing river
>   that laves the rootlets
>   of those sweet-scented flowers
> that people the
>   milky
>   way   .

Here the triadic verse seems to give out rather than break down, as if Char's stream had run dry in his admirer: Williams has no images of natural beauty of his own that might nourished by its waters. Instead, as with his observation of the unicorn tapestry, beauty achieved summons troubling memories of unredeemed animal pain, a childhood dog he once kicked in alarm, thinking that her pups "were biting her breasts | to destroy her," and a rabbit, "lying harmlessly | on the outspread palm | of a hunter's hand," who, as Williams watched, "took a hunting knife | and with a laugh | thrust it | up into the animal's private parts" (2:255–56).

Williams rarely uses anaphora to organize the stanzas of his triadic poems, and his use of it here—"I remember Norma | our English setter of my childhood . . . I remember also | a dead rabbit" (2:255–56)—formalizes the operations of memory as a choric response to present pain. The traumatic moments from childhood do not appear immediately, as an involuntary response to the dog's injury; rather, Williams invokes and stages them with some deliberation as a kind of litany over the dying animal that is provoked by the thought of what Char might have done in his place. The performance agrees with Adam Smith's assertion that physical pain demands an exchange of narratives if it is to become sympathy: the child's shock when confronted by things it had not known to be a part of its world is what allows us to imagine how the unexpected catastrophe that has overtaken the dog might feel to the animal itself.

The dying dog challenges Williams, via Char, to give an account of his art's responsibilities, and he does so in exemplary fashion, finding narratives from his own life that enable his readers to approach what the animal experiences in its death. It is an admirable demonstration of how human beings might come to sympathize with nonhuman pain, but the poem does not end here. Instead, Williams follows the stories from his childhood with a question that undermines the function they have just been called upon to perform—"Why should I think of that now?"—and an assertion that seems to undo the poem we have just been reading: "The cries of a dying dog | are to be blotted out | as best I can." If the appropriate response to the animal's pain was to try to blot it out, why was the poem written in the first place?

The answer requires returning to Char, this time in an effort to give an explicit account of his poetics, rather than an acknowledgment of them that exhausts itself in failed imitation of the poems they inform (2:257):

> René Char
> you are a poet who believes
> in the power of beauty
> to right all wrongs.
> I believe it also.
> With invention and courage
> we shall surpass
> the pitiful dumb beasts,
> let all men believe it,
> as you have taught me also
> to believe it.

"Invention" occurs as a programmatic term in a long manifesto-like passage of *Paterson*—"Without invention nothing is well spaced" (50)—in which it signals an intention to move beyond inherited structures of thought, verse, and feeling, in an effort to open cultural activity to the present and the local situation. Here it is coupled with courage, but in a gesture of self-cancellation: this poem is not an example of the poetics to which it aspires. While Williams shares Char's belief in beauty's power to right wrongs, his own poem has not been beautiful. Instead of surpassing the "pitiful dumb beasts," it has exhibited a dumbness akin to theirs. It has been full of ugliness, and it has stammered out its message in odd forms of recursion, rather than stating it clearly and beautifully.

The failure of invention in "To a Dog Injured in the Street" is another glance at the poetics of *Paterson*, more fleeting than the reprinting of "The descent beckons" with which *The Desert Music* opens, but a reconsideration of the poetics of iambic incapacity nonetheless. While the dog poet of the earlier work sought out his descent into the nonhuman, the poet of the latter book can no longer rise above it; he can imagine forms of human achievement that will surpass "the pitiful dumb beasts," but his own is not one of them: his poem stages and acknowledges the same inability to turn suffering into beauty that is formalized in Hipponax's broken line.

In the collections that follow *The Desert Music—Journey to Love* and *Pictures from Brueghel*—aggression returns as an occasion for Williams's cathexis to other animals, but it is now paired with vulnerability as its ever present counterpart, so that the body of any animal documents the energies it has expended in pursuit of its preferred activities. In "The Sparrow," Williams begins with a species level admiration for the bird's unabashed identification with its own sexuality (2:292):

> Wherever he finds himself
> in early spring,
> on back streets
> or beside palaces,
> he carries on
> unaffectedly
> his amours.
> It begins in the egg,
> his sex genders it:
> What is more pretentiously
> useless
> or about which
> we more pride ourselves?
> It leads as often as not
> to our undoing.

Here we might seem to have returned to the dog poet as Cynic: the animal does in plain view what human beings hypocritically disavow. Williams's praise of the sparrow's unaffectedness does not, however, entail a contrast between instinctual behavior in the bird and second-order self-consciousness in human beings. For the sparrow's amours, as Williams sees them, are a deliberately enacted behavior—something it "carries on"—and, as such, are nuanced from one individual to another: he recalls seeing a female catch a male by his crown-feathers and hold him "silent,| subdued,| hanging above the city streets | until | she was through with him" (2:294).

Williams does not proclaim generalized laws of animal behavior, so that human beings can be satirized for diverging from them, but looks instead for actions in which the characteristics of individual animals manifest themselves against the background of norms for their species. From such observation there emerges a consideration of how it is that one's own experience comes to take on a distinctive shape, recognizable to oneself and to others as a life lived by a particular individual. Williams remembers being puzzled by the female's success, as he claims the bird herself was, and he moves suddenly from her unexpected triumph to the dead sparrow lying before him in the street, "a wisp of feathers | flattened to the pavement" (2:294). The "black escutcheon" of its breast appears "undecipherable" to him at first, but the memory of the idiosyncratic female calls forth an effort to interpret this "effigy of a sparrow" as what must have been an individual too.

Williams sees the sparrow's death in a public street as a sign that it remained "practical to the end," and, given this evidence that the bird pursued its characteristic pleasures even unto death, he claims in response to its ruined and abandoned body that "it is the poem | of his existence | that triumphed finally" (2:294). The sparrow's body is "the poem of his existence" not only in the restrictive sense that it is the only testimony to itself the bird is able to offer, but also because this testimony is as distinctive as any individual body is to the person who can read it as the badge of a life:

This was I,
          a sparrow.
               I did my best;
farewell.

The "dried wafer" of the sparrow's body is a unique disposal of the conative energies common to its species. It is made apprehensible as such by a verse form that is itself both a generic achievement and a register of particularity. The poem gives out suddenly on "farewell," but unabashedly, even triumphantly so, like the animal whose life it imagines. It is this discernibility of individual accomplishment against a generic background that makes the sparrow's body legible as the record of an individual life, and Williams's poem a successful testimony to it, so that the two can be analogized as particular forms of the expressive behavior in which the existence of human beings and other animals is spent.[43]

Williams's teasing out of analogy in "The Sparrow" requires the deliberate evocation of memories of species observation to combat the appearance of indecipherability the bird's remains present.[44] Imagination is enabled by obstacle and the exiguousness of the material with which it has to work. Its operations here contrast with the full-bore imaginative identification with animal aggression in "The Turtle," a poem from Williams's last collection, *Pictures from Brueghel*. "The Turtle" is written for the poet's grandson, as "The Sparrow" is dedicated to his father, and it stages a twofold movement of sympathy as the poet thinks himself into the animal through the strange fascination it exerts over the child. This fascination consists mostly in the capacity to inflict harm the child imagines the turtle to possess (2:432–33):

> Not because of his eyes,
> > the eyes of a bird,
> > > but because he is beaked,
> birdlike, to do an injury,
> > has the turtle attracted you.
> > > He is your only pet.

The child is not interested in the life that shows in the animal's eyes, but in the armored exterior that may at any moment rupture the boredom of adult conversations with a deadly assault:[45]

43. Cf. Haraway (2008, 27–30), who objects to Deleuze and Guattari's account of "becoming animal" for ignoring the individuality of nonhuman animals in its fantasies of the pack and the herd. Williams notes that social groups of sparrows may number in the tens of thousands, but such groups are the background against which the characteristics of individual animals are discerned, not the horizon into which they merge.

44. Williams wrote seven poems about sparrows, the others being "Pastoral" (1:20), "The Sleeping Brute" (2:11), "Sparrows Among Dry Leaves" (2:91), "To a Sparrow" (2:100), "Passer Domesticus" (2:237), and "Sappho, Be Comforted" (2:433).

45. This aspect of "becoming animal" in Kafka's stories—a kind of jubilant, childlike protest against the tedium of adult life—is well described by Deleuze and Guattari: "To become a beetle, to become a dog, to become an ape . . . rather than lowering one's head and remaining a bureaucrat, inspector, judge, or judged. All children build or feel these sorts of escapes, these acts of becoming-animal" (1986, 12).

When we are together
> you talk of nothing else
>> ascribing all sorts
of murderous motives
> to his least action.
>> You ask me
to write a poem,
> should I have poems to write,
>> about a turtle.

Williams is ostensibly writing about his grandson's desire for the aggressive energy he locates in the turtle, but the poet's own aggression surfaces here too. He knows his own fragility holds no appeal for the child, and the requested poem within the poem begins with the suggestion that his grandson's pet might prefer to unleash its cataclysmic destruction on the world without its owner's company:

When he shall escape
> his present confinement
he will stride about the world
> destroying all
>> with his sharp beak.
Whatever opposes him
> in the streets of the city
>> shall go down.
Cars will be overturned.
> And upon his back
>> shall ride,
to his conquests,
> my Lord,
>> you!

Williams delays gratification of his grandson's fantasies until the final word of this visionary havoc, whereupon the turtle morphs just as suddenly into an altogether different animal:

In the beginning
> there was a great tortoise
who supported the world.

Upon him
            all ultimately
rests.
Without him
            nothing will stand.
He is all wise
            and can outrun the hare.
                        In the night
his eyes carry him
            to unknown places.
                        He is your friend.

The great tortoise is a composite figure. "In the beginning" echoes the biblical God's priority to his own Creation, even as Williams recalls the Turtle Island of American Indian cosmogony: the earth accumulating slowly on the back of a turtle swimming in the ocean.[46] He has the patience of Aesop's tortoise, but also the speed to beat the hare in a footrace. He is supremely sagacious, but still curious about the universe that is himself. A child is asked to believe in his benevolence.

Williams gestures at a poetic materialism, in which poetry's myth making would reconcile us to the universe by making the transitions between animate and inanimate being imaginatively bearable.[47] But the tortoise is not a philosophical or religious system, even one for children. Like Peter the Dwarf, he is the epiphany of an immediate imaginative need, both urgent and local, a face glimpsed in the trees, or the momentary apprehension of a figure in the stars. It is on this understanding that he is handed back to the child with an injunction to trust in the bricolage that he is.

"The Turtle" fulfills the trajectory of Williams's iambic poetics by asking us to consider whether the end of animate embodiment in death is a fact the

46. Williams may even have in mind what is purportedly a Hindu myth, often invoked in theories of infinite regress, from Locke's *An Essay Concerning Human Understanding* to Stephen Hawking's *A Brief History of Time*: the world rests on an elephant, which in turn rests on a tortoise, or turtle. To the question, "What does the turtle rest on?" the answer can only be: "It's turtles all the way down." The key passages can be found at http://en.wikipedia.org/wiki/Turtles_all_the_way_down, and I thank Joshua Scodel for bringing this reference to my attention.

47. Cf. Riddel (1974, 52–53), and Schuster (2007, 116–17), who suggests that the "radical redistribution" in such entropic processes as potlatch appears as a model for the poetic imagination's "breakdown of the human" as early as *Spring and All*.

animate human subject can imaginatively embrace. Beyond the continuities with animal life grasped in the experiences of wounding and vulnerability lies the body's return to the "granular stench" of its own matter. The tortoise infinitely strong and infinitely extensive subsumes the dead and dying animals of Williams's later poetry, but the answer he gives to the poem's imaginative question is as tenuous as their matter's configuration into life. The fragility of the figure by which the turtle of unlimited aggression becomes the tortoise of unlimited sagacity instantiates the precariousness of the imaginative work it invites us to undertake.

CHAPTER TWO

Destruction and Creation

The Work of Men and Animals in Gustave Flaubert,
Gerard Manley Hopkins, and Ezra Pound

Destruction was my Beatrice. —Stéphane Mallarmé

In the previous chapter, I looked at aggression as a mode of cathexis to non-human animals and the forms of human self-understanding this cathexis enabled. In this chapter, I want to look at aggression toward other animals and the forms of human self-understanding this aggression occludes. In particular, I will consider the relationship between aggression and ontological narcissism in fictions of unlimited destructiveness, and I will argue that these fictions are versions of the myth of Satanism, in which hatred of other kinds of life than one's own grounds the desire to destroy them. Finally, by contrast, I will examine some accounts of poetic labor that fashion an escape from such narcissism in the acknowledgment of continuity between the work of poets and the work of other animals.

Herman Melville, in *Moby-Dick*, ponders the sperm whale's chances of avoiding extermination in "polar citadels," where, unlike with the bison of the American plains, they might escape the lethal attention of his countrymen:

> Comparing the humped herds of whales with the humped herds of buffalo, which, not forty years ago, overspread by tens of thousands the prairies of Illinois and Missouri, and shook their iron manes and scowled with their thunder-clotted brows upon the sites of populous river-capitals, where now the polite broker sells you land at a dollar an inch; in such a comparison an irresistible argument would seem furnished, to show that the hunted whale cannot now escape speedy extinc-

tion. But you must look at this matter in every light. Though so short a period ago—not a good life-time—the census of the buffalo in Illinois exceeded the census of men now in London, and though at the present day not one horn or hoof of them remains in all that region; and though the cause of this wondrous extermination was the spear of man; yet the far different nature of the whale-hunt peremptorily forbids so inglorious an end to the Leviathan. Forty men in one ship hunting the Sperm Whale for forty-eight months think they have done extremely well, and thank God, if at last they carry home the oil of forty fish. Whereas, in the days of the old Canadian and Indian hunters and trappers of the West, when the far west (in whose sunset suns still rise) was a wilderness and a virgin, the same number of moccasined men, for the same number of months, mounted on horse instead of sailing in ships, would have slain not forty, but forty thousand and more buffaloes; a fact that, if need were, could be statistically stated. (105:573).[1]

Melville is prescient in calling the days of bison hunting on a massive scale the old days in *Moby-Dick*. In 1851, the numbers of American bison were not yet seeing the catastrophic decline that occurred between 1870 and 1890, but the overhunting that was to reduce a population estimated at between twenty-five and thirty million at the time of the arrival of the first Europeans to a few hundred animals by the end of the century could already be discerned.[2] The bison, once the most numerous of large American fauna, narrowly escaped the fate of the passenger pigeon, which went from being the most numerous American bird, with numbers estimated at between three and five billion at the time of the European arrival, to complete extinction in September 1914, when the last captive bird died in a Cincinnati zoo. As with the bison, a massive acceleration in their decline occurred between 1870 and 1890, as industrial methods enabled the slaughter of tens of thousands of birds at a time. The revival of the species from small numbers of captive animals that allowed conservationists to prevent the extinction of the bison proved ineffective in the case of the passenger pigeon, as the birds did not reproduce when the large flocks in which they had once lived were destroyed.[3]

1. Melville (1972, 105:573). All citations of *Moby-Dick* are from this edition. To facilitate reference to other editions, I have included both chapter number and page number, separated by a colon.
2. See Isenberg 2000, 3–25, 65–66, 143–62.
3. See http://en.wikipedia.org/wiki/Passenger_Pigeon. As Leopold put it on the monument to the passenger pigeon in Wyalusing State Park, Wisconsin, the bird "could survive no dimi-

As the American slaughter was proceeding apace, Gustave Flaubert was writing his short story "La légende de saint Julien L'Hospitalier." Set in a fabulous version of the Middle Ages, it tells the tale of a young man driven to wander the earth by his inability to understand himself as a part of it. Julien is born in a fairy-tale castle to parents who love and cherish him, but he is set upon a career of destruction by the sight of a mouse that appears unexpectedly at Mass one day. He kills it without knowing why, throwing away its body, then begins to kill birds with stones and, in due course, devotes himself to the life of a hunter, in which the irrational destructiveness that lies behind his pursuits is signaled by such pointless and fantastic acts of cruelty as cutting off the legs of a sleeping grouse.[4]

Julien revels not just in killing every kind of animal but in exterminating every member of every group of animals he encounters. In one scene, he finds himself before a valley "shaped like an amphitheater and filled with stags." The animals are "crowded close together, warming each other with their breath," and Julien kills every one of them before leaning his back against a tree, and "considering with wide-eyed wonderment the magnitude of the slaughter, unable to understand how he could have carried it out" (66–67). The last stag Julien kills warns him that he will be punished by killing his own parents, so he flees to an exotic marriage in a foreign land, where he relives his slaughter in his dreams. He sees himself "like our father Adam in the middle of Paradise with all the birds and animals around him," but his self-appointed task in Eden is not to name, but to kill, the animals. And he kills in a dream of effortless ease; merely by "stretching out his arm, he would put them to death," or "from the shadow of a cave he would hurl javelins at them which never missed their aim" (72).

Eventually persuaded by his noble kinsmen to return to the chase, Julien finds himself surrounded by the eyes of mysterious animals that can't be killed, so that "he cursed out loud, spoiling for a fight, howling imprecations, choking with rage" (77). They are the ghosts of all the animals he has killed, and they drive him back to his palace, where he inadvertently kills his parents, who have arrived in his absence after long years of searching for their lost son during which they have become wretched, unrecognizable beggars. Julien now begins his penance, in which he ceases from wandering, oper-

---

nution of his own furious intensity" (1949, 111): its extinction was made inevitable by wanton extermination of the last few large flocks, even when it was clear this would mean doom for the species.

4. Flaubert 1961, 65.

ates a free river ferry for travelers, and is finally taken up to Heaven by Christ, around Whom, in the form of a destitute leper, he has been willing to wrap his own naked body.

The fairy-tale manner of Flaubert's story, the outlines of which we are told at the conclusion have been drawn from a stained glass window in a local church, wills timelessness upon its themes of existential homelessness, biocidal destructiveness, and redemption by divine intervention. Julien's only respite from his career of destruction comes when he sequesters himself in his wife's Moorish palace. This building, which stands alone on an isolated promontory, is a haven of mineral delights that cloisters its inhabitants from the life world beyond:

> The walls were full of shadow, but received some light from the inlaid decorations of the walls. Tall columns, as slender as reeds, supported the domes, which were adorned with reliefs imitating the stalactites which are to be found in grottoes. There were fountains in the main rooms, mosaics in the courtyards, festooned walls, countless architectural refinements, and everywhere a silence so profound that one could hear rustle of a scarf or the echo of a sigh. (71–72)

Flaubert's description of the palace is a perfect capsule of Symbolist aesthetics not simply because of its Orientalism, but because of the way in which this Orientalism imagines aesthetic pleasure to involve a thorough exclusion of what is alive. These are minerals as "the least frightening of all existents," as Jean-Paul Sartre was to put it in *Nausea*,[5] and the stones of Julien's refuge draw a sharp line between the enjoyment of lifeless materials and the horror of warm bodies that fills him with murderous rage.

Julien's palace has its analogues in Baudelaire's "La Beauté" ("Beauty"), naked "like a dream of stone," and the concomitant conception of the erotic as an escape from human animality: the eyes of a dancer seduce because they are "made of charming minerals" and they open upon a space in which "everything is gold, steel, light and diamonds"; their allure is that of the sterile woman who shines "like a useless star" ("Avec ses vêtements ondoyants et nacrés"). By contrast, the raucous forest of "Obsession" terrifies "like a cathedral" because it reminds the poet that his desire to escape Nature is itself the mark of a fallen nature that wants to believe itself uncreated. Only the ocean is to be cherished; an abyss "no less bitter" than the human spirit, and no less in

---

5. Cited in Harrison 1992, 148.

love with "carnage and death," it is mankind's mirror, wherein he may distract himself for a while with rumors of a savagery greater than his own ("L'homme et la mer").

Baudelaire systematically equates inorganicism with Satanism, and Mallarmé maintains the psychic structure of this equation while dropping the trappings of Christianity. Faced, in "L'azur," with the choice between a Sky that is dead, and the "human livestock" that sleep on the ground, the poet hears the metal of church bells as the summoning of an anti-naturalism he dare not refuse: "Où fuir dans la révolte inutile et perverse? | *Je suis hanté.* L'Azur! l'Azur! l'Azur! l'Azur!" Mallarmé's exclamations are the birth pangs of a Satanism that no longer has God the creator, but only Nature, to rebel against.

The Symbolist equation of inorganicism and Satanism has good literary foundations. In *Paradise Lost*, Satan's first act after his expulsion from Heaven is to build—or rather, to have built for him—the infernal city of Pandemonium (1.713–30):

> Built like a temple, where pilasters round
> Were set, and Doric pillars overlaid
> With golden architrave; nor did there want
> Cornice or frieze, with bossy sculptures graven:
> The roof was fretted gold. Not Babylon
> Nor great Al-cairo such magnificence
> Equaled in all their glories, to enshrine
> Belus or Serapis their gods, or seat
> Their kings, when Egypt with Assyria strove
> In wealth and luxury. The ascending pile
> Stood fixed her stately height; and straight the doors
> Opening their brazen folds, discover, wide
> Within, her ample spaces o'er the smooth
> And level pavement: from the arched roof,
> Pendent by subtle magic, many a row
> Of starry lamps and blazing cressets, fed
> With naphtha and asphaltus, yielded light
> As from a sky.

Satan's palace is the model for all earthly palaces, although Oriental ones copy their great prototype most faithfully. Lest we think Satan builds with inorganic materials out of sheer necessity—what else is there in Hell?—

Milton reminds us that what he makes is a grim parody of Heaven, whose "crystal battlements" and pavement of "trodden gold" the devils ape with metal, stone, and artificial light.

From this perspective, humankind's feats of architectural engineering are no more than second order Satanism, rooted in envy of the unnaturalness that is appropriate to Heaven, but the sign of a perverted will to believe in an exemption from the conditions of createdness on the part of fallen angels and fallen human beings. In Paradise, Adam and Eve recline on a "soft downy bank damasked with flowers" (4.334); when an angel visits them, they eat fruits on "mossy seats" at a table of "grassy turf" (5.391–92). Human infatuation with inorganic materials begins with the Fall. It compounds the first disobedience by misunderstanding human difference as the possibility for absolute separation from the rest of Creation and trying to live accordingly.[6]

RESENTMENT AS THE GROUND OF HUMAN DESTRUCTIVENESS

In *Paradise Lost*, Satan travels from Pandemonium to Eden to see human beings and the world God has made for them. Milton tells us that "the fiend | Saw undelighted all delight, all kind | Of living creatures new to sight and strange" (4.285–87). There is, however, a certain amount of editorializing in this claim. What Satan himself tells us is that his thoughts pursue the creatures of Paradise, human beings included, "with wonder," and that he "could love" them (4.362–63): Satan admires other forms of life, but admiration, instead of leading him to love, leads him to hate and destroy the very sights that inspire it.

6. Harrison begins his history of human gardening with the mineral "garden of the gods" (2008, 1) in *The Epic of Gilgamesh*. Like Pindar's Island of the Blessed, with its flowers of blazing gold (*Olympian* 2.72), this garden, with its fruits of carnelian and leaves of lapis lazuli, is for immortals only and confirms Milton's suggestion that a strong preference for the inorganic among human beings is likely a sign of overreaching and forgetfulness of the mortal condition. A version of this category error is an occasion for hilarity in Ovid's story of Philemon and Baucis (*Metamorphoses* 8.611–724). As a reward to the old man and his wife, who, alone of their kind, have shown hospitality to Jupiter and Mercury disguised as human beings, the gods inundate the countryside around their home, drowning all its inhabitants except the happy couple, and stranding the house itself on an isolated promontory, where the thatched, wood-framed cottage, with its bed of willow and sedge and cups of earthenware and beech wood, is transformed into a splendid temple with a golden roof and marble floor. In Ovid's whimsical Golden Age narrative, it is the gods themselves who propel the last pious human beings from a life of harmony with nature into a world of luxury and opulence.

Satan says that his eyes "with grief behold, | Into our room of bliss thus high advanced | Creatures of other mould" (4.358-60). He uses the plural—"our room"—to speak of his own kind, even though he is soliloquizing here; he is pained to find other kinds of beings in a place he feels ought to belong to his kind alone, and he suffers their presence as a kind of ontological chastisement. The pattern is repeated when he returns to Paradise in Book 9 to carry out his plan to destroy it. "With what delight could I have walked thee round, | If I could joy in aught," he exclaims (9.114-15), and he points to the features of Eden's natural diversity as each one a source of pain, since he is excluded from them all (9.115-21):

> Sweet interchange
> Of hill and valley, rivers, woods, and plains,
> Now land, now sea, and shores with forest crowned,
> Rocks, dens, and caves; but I in none of these
> Find place of refuge; and the more I see
> Pleasures about me, so much more I feel
> Torment within me.

The earth is home to animals and as yet unfallen human beings, but not to Satan; resenting his homelessness, he imagines destroying what he sees: "For only in destroying I find ease | To my relentless thoughts" (9.129-30). Satan turns his destructiveness into a plot, projecting glory for himself in marring God's work (9.136-37), but this construal of his urge to destroy as vengeance is a second-order response: his destructiveness flows directly from the intensity of his resentment that there is something in the world beside his own kind and is only afterwards given narrative shape.

Works of fiction generally have individuals as their protagonists, but Milton, like Flaubert, points to the level of generality at which his narrative is to be understood. Satan speaks for his kind, not merely for himself, and his resentment of other life is categorical: he resents the creatures God has fashioned to live on Earth because they remind him that the class of beings to which he belongs is unexceptional in its createdness. As a fictional particular representing the psychic functions of a collective identity, Satan, like Julien, has much to tell us about human homelessness and human beings' hostility to the other forms of life with which they share their world. For Satan's destructiveness, exemplary of the destructiveness of his kind toward the other beings whose presence in the world they resent, will become the destructiveness of fallen humankind toward the other creatures whose mortality they will soon share and whose presence is a perpetual reminder of their former exemption from this condition.[7]

Susan Howe, in her poem of the Puritan experience of the New England forest, *Articulation of Sound Forms in Time*, calls this collective aggression "destructivism":

> Colonnades of rigorous Americanism
> Portents of lonely destructivism[8]

Howe's term is more telling than "destruction," which names consequences, "will to destroy," which locates the urge at a higher level of intentionality than that at which it operates, and even "destructiveness," which might suggest accidental blundering. "Destructivism" names the pattern of human behavior that begins as a feeling of homelessness, then turns to wandering, resentment of the natural world expressed as inorganicism ("Colonnades of rigorous Americanism"), and, finally, an urge to destroy what cannot be embraced as home. It is operative at a collective level, but is not enjoyed by the members of the collective as an activity in which they feel themselves to be participating together: the narratives of Julien and Satan are as lonely as Howe's, even as they represent the psychic functions of a group.

Destructivism, then, would seem to be a good counter-term to what E. O. Wilson has called biophilia, the human species' "innate pleasure from living abundance and diversity."[9] Wilson adopted the term from Erich Fromm, in whose work "biophilia" is paired with "necrophilia," so as to form a contrast between "the passionate love of life and of all that is alive," expressed in the desire to nourish growth, whether of persons, plants, ideas, or social groups, and the pathological abhorrence of the living that has among its symptoms solipsistic destructiveness and fetishization of the inorganic.[10] For Fromm,

7. Cf. Harrison on *Gilgamesh*: "There is too often a deliberate rage and vengefulness at work in the assault on nature and its species, as if one would project onto the natural world the intolerable anxieties of finitude which hold humanity hostage to death" (1992, 18). Harrison's account nicely captures the movement of a psychic force that begins with the individual ("one") but gathers momentum as it considers the fate of the species as a whole ("humanity hostage to death").

8. Howe (1987). The text is unpaginated, but this quote can be found in the section entitled "Hope Atherton's Wanderings."

9. Wilson (1998, 212). Earlier definitions by Wilson include "the innate tendency to focus on life and lifelike processes" and the "urge to affiliate with other forms of life" (1984, 1), and "the innately emotional affiliation of human beings to other living organisms" (1993, 33).

10. Fromm 1973, 342–45, 398.

the longing for what is not alive originates in human beings' alienation from other animals. The sense human beings have that they are "not at home in nature" and "evicted from paradise" (225) leads them to fashion an alternative world of artifacts in which they do feel at home, and, by a feedback loop, these objects reinforce the feelings of exceptionalism that led to their production in the first place.

For both Fromm and Wilson, human culture originates in an aversion from other forms of life, and its collective appeal continues to lie, to one degree or another, in its ability to foster solipsistic fantasies of categorical difference.[11] Fromm's belief that this culture of narcissistic aversion will have destructiveness as one of its forms closely tracks Milton's account of the emergence of Satan's destructiveness in *Paradise Lost*. For, in Milton's poem, Death is born from Satan's infatuation with his own self-image in Sin—"Thyself in me thy perfect image viewing | Becam'st enamored" (2.764–65), as She puts it—and it is the primal destructiveness that emerges from this narcissism and manifests itself in the War in Heaven that is traumatically repeated in Satan's urge to destroy the other beings he finds in Eden.

Many accounts of narcissistic destructiveness seek its origins in developmental trauma,[12] but Satan's narcissism is an existential mystery. Even Raphael, in his account of the bad angels' rebellion, will not approach it more closely as a psychic event than to say that Satan "thought himself impaired" by God's elevation of his Son, before moving immediately on to describe the outcome of this mistaken understanding in Satan's "deep malice" and "disdain" (5.665–66). For Raphael at least, no one wounds Satan, and his inability to accept that he is one kind of being among others can be witnessed in

11. Wilson is more radical in this respect, claiming not merely that culture provides human beings with a world other than nature in which to feel at home, but that the world it offers is always in some sense narcissistic wish fulfillment, given that artifacts can only be "a mirror to our thoughts." See Wilson (1984, 115), and compare with the discussion of how Wilson's concept of biophilia differs from Fromm's in Orr (1993, 415–16).

12. So Naess imagines a "destructive urge addressed to the whole world and existence as such" as the outcome of "severe tragedy" in childhood that interrupts a developmental process that would otherwise lead to "positive feeling to all of nature through the insight that everything is interconnected" (1989, 164), and Neville Symington sees turning away from sources of nourishment outside the self and the resulting inability to acknowledge dependency on others as the outcome of childhood situations in which "extreme emotional pain is coupled with a lack of the empathetic, thoughtful attention that would make the pain bearable." See the discussion in Nicholsen (2002, 57–58). Even Melville's Ahab, modeled after Milton's Satan in the many ways noted in Sheldon (2002, 38–39), loathes other forms of life because of the wound Moby-Dick has inflicted on him.

the kind of being that he is, but not explained with reference to the actions of an outside agent. While God's actions may be the occasion for Satan's destructiveness, they are no more its cause than the mouse that provokes Flaubert's Julien to kill every living thing in his path is the cause of his career of slaughter.

BEYOND NARCISSISM

Satan's infatuation with his own self-image in Sin represents the possibility for an unlimited and unimpeded cycle of transference and countertransference, a compounding exaltation of solipsistic self-understanding that is never disturbed by comparison with what is not himself. When he is obliged to interrupt this cloistered composure of selfhood and attend to other forms of life, discerning appreciation of what is other than his own kind is not lacking, but issues in relentless and unlimited destructiveness.

Man the exterminator is by now a familiar figure of historical ecology: total extirpation of insular bird species by pre-European settlers of New Zealand and Hawaii is well documented, and there seems to be some evidence that the prehistoric extinction of most species of large American and Australian mammals, like the nineteenth-century slaughter of the bison and passenger pigeon, was also caused by unstinting human predation, even in the face of its obviously deleterious effects upon the human communities that perpetuated it.[13] Narcissistic aversion from other forms of life has even been proposed as the cause of this unchecked aggression.[14] As God reminds Job, human vanity

---

13. See Diamond (1992, 317–38) and Leakey (1995, 171–94). As they note, the American evidence remains controversial.

14. Shepard, in a discussion of Julia Kristeva's reading of the myth of Narcissus, locates its emergence in the transition from the life of the hunter gatherer to the life of agriculture: as human beings replaced the "mosaic of wild fauna" on which they depended for their survival with sustenance of their own making, they exchanged an image of themselves pieced together from "shared elements in the context of otherness" for the pursuit of a perfect self-image derived from themselves alone (1993, 293–95). Diamond (1992, 296) questions Fromm's belief in self-imposed limits upon destructive aggression in hunter-gather societies, but Indian observers consistently attribute the destructiveness of white bison killers to demonic or childish narcissism over and above the obvious intention to deprive them of the herds on which their way of life depended: "You can see that the men who did this are crazy, they just killed and killed because they liked to do that" (Black Elk, Oglala); "Have the white men become children, that they should kill meat and not eat" (Satanta, Kiowa); "We thought that these people must be devils, for they had no sympathy" (Luther Standing Bear, Lakota) (cited in Calloway 1996, 123–26).

is limited only by the technologies of destruction with which it is inscribed on the rest of Creation: "Canst thou draw out leviathan with an hook? or his tongue with a cord which thou lettest down? Canst thou put an hook into his nose? or bore his jaw through with a thorn?" (Job 41:1–2).

Under what circumstances does interrupted identification with self-image produce sympathetic attentiveness to what interrupts it instead of narcissistic destructivism? As we shall see in the next chapter, Melville suggests in *Moby-Dick* that human beings are slow to perceive individuality in large populations of others animals: Ishmael at first regards the social groups of whales he sees as little more than lumps of matter suspended in the ocean, and it is only by spending a long time looking closely at a single severed head that he begins to perceive that he is hunting individuals, with particular histories, and particular bodies, in which can be discerned the same inextricable combination of personality, heredity, and circumstance that shapes human lives. Environmental and conservation groups likewise typically attempt to leverage singularity as a mechanism that enables sympathetic identification with the members of endangered species:[15] the American bison was saved from complete extermination by becoming the charismatic megafauna of its day, and even Martha, the last passenger pigeon, became an individual on the brink of her species' extinction, painted, photographed, and even filmed in the months before her death.

Satan, however, should caution against undue reliance upon scarcity as a way of bringing about a transition from the perception of generality in other animals to a perception of particularity with the power to arrest the pursuits in which they figure as no more than matter for human use: there are, after all, only two human beings in the Eden he visits. In what follows, therefore, I want to consider instances of such perceptual change that are not provoked by the prospect of total annihilation of the objects of perception in order to consider how everyday appreciation of the lives of other animals might reduce the need for such emergency thinking.

The scholastic terms for the perceptual change Ishmael undergoes are *quidditas* ("whatness" or generality) and *haecceitas* ("thisness," or particularity). So Martin Heidegger claims that the perception of a common "treeness" in oaks, beeches, birches, and firs, for example, was an essential precondition for the development of technologies in which they figure as mere

15. See, for example, the rationale behind the WWF's flagship species at http://www.panda .org/about_our_earth/species/about_species/flagship_keystone_indicator_definition/index .cfm.

lumber.[16] Conversely, Gerard Manley Hopkins makes the ability to perceive *haecceitas*—what distinguishes one aspen tree from another—a precondition for the kind of writing about other living things that might shield them from reckless destruction at the hands of human beings.

Hopkins began to think about *haecceitas* after reading the medieval theologian Duns Scotus, but the idea of "inscape" he developed from this reading is not identical with Scotus's concept. Hopkins gave the name "inscape" to the fully realized perception of "thisness," and "instress" to the state in which the perceiver dwells in or with this perception.[17] The term "inscape," in fact, first appears in Hopkins's notes for a lecture on Parmenides. Heraclitus, whose influence is explicit in Hopkins's most ambitious title—"That Nature is a Heraclitean Fire and of the Comfort of the Resurrection"—may have been important, too; the definition of "inscape" in his journal entry of February 24, 1873—"all the world is full of inscape and chance left free to act falls into an order as well as purpose"[18]—precedes a description of "random clods and broken heaps of snow made by the cast of a broom," and this combination of image and assertion is strikingly reminiscent of Heraclitus fragment 125: "the most beautiful order is a pile swept up at random."[19]

Hopkins's journal entry of August 10, 1872, describes the emergence of instress from inscape as a kind of expansive accommodation of the human eye to the nonhuman life it observes:

> Green-white tufts of long bleached grass like heads of hair or the crowns of heads of hair, each a whorl of slender curves, one tuft taking up another—however these I might have noticed any day. I saw the inscape though freshly, as if my eye were still growing, though with a companion the eye and the ear are for the most part shut and instress cannot come.[20]

16. Heidegger (1977a, 29). Heidegger presumably chooses trees as his example because of the ancient connection between words for wood and words for matter, or material (Greek *hyle*, Latin *materia*); compare this with the treatment of *hyle* in the discussion of matter and form in "The Origin of the Work of Art" (Heidegger 1971, 26–30) and the thoughtful reflection on the ancient forest's transformation into matter in Harrison (1992, 27–28).

17. See Ballinger (2000, 103–18, 129n65), who offers the intriguing suggestion that for Hopkins, who became increasingly interested in etymology over the course of his life, "inscape" may have been "a cognate of the Greek verb *skopein* (to look attentively) or the noun *skopos* (that upon which one fixes his or her look)" (52).

18. Hopkins 1953, 128.

19. Kahn 1979, 85.

20. Hopkins (1953, 127). All of Hopkins's poems cited in this chapter are from this edition.

The journal entry suggests that solitude is virtually a requirement for the experience of instress, and, in the poem "Binsey Poplars" (39–40), Hopkins explores the limits of its communicability as a transformative encounter with other forms of life. The poem laments the destruction of a row of poplar trees that lined a riverbank at Binsey, near Oxford. Hopkins gives the date of their death in the manner of a human epitaph—"felled 1879" appears immediately below the poem's title—and goes on to remember what the trees had been, how they "dandled a sandaled | Shadow that swam or sank | On meadow and river and wind-wandering weed-winding bank." The effort at remembering precedes an assertion of human ignorance—"O if we but knew what we do | When we delve or hew"—and the claim that the place in which the trees grew has been ruined forever by their destruction: their felling is to the scene as a whole what a pin prick would be to the "sleek and seeing ball" of the human eye.

Since the trees were what was looked at by the poet, comparing them to the "seeing ball" of the human eye is a surprising reversal of agency. But it is this reversal that reveals the encounter with "thisness" as transactional, or even intersubjective—something other than an idle onlooker gazing distractedly at whatever meets his eyes. For Hopkins follows the claim that the landscape has been blinded by the destruction of the trees with an assertion that annuls the memorializing power of his own first stanza: "After-comers cannot guess the beauty been." How is it, we must now ask, that we cannot guess the poplars' beauty from the poem we are reading? Surely that is exactly what the evocative description of their airy branches has just allowed us to do, preserving them for readers so that nothing, we might think, has been lost by their transmutation into artifacts of human culture?

In the final lines of the poem, Hopkins tells us that "Strokes of havoc únselve | The sweet especial scene," and that this "sweet especial scene" was a "rural scene." The repetition is insistent: "Rural scene, a rural scene, | Sweet especial rural scene." What we must ask about, then, is the nature of the personhood Hopkins claims for the trees with his coinage "únselve," and what it was about their rural location that allowed them to manifest this personhood in a way that has called for memorialization, even if such memorialization has proved inadequate to the experience of the trees themselves.

The rural scene in which the poplars grew was likely close to fields in which agricultural work was done, but it is clear that the trees themselves were not objects of human cultivation. On the riverbank where they "dandled a sandaled | Shadow" they grew freely and were able to attain their distinctive shapes and behave in their characteristic ways without human interference.

Their movement with the water was genuinely self-expressive, dependent upon particular environmental features, but not subject to human training and control. The scene was a pocket of wilderness in the midst of human culture and so could hail the passerby with a show of life untouched by human hands. It is for this reason that the poplars were irreplaceable, and why a poem, which is a work of human hands, can provide what the trees gave to the encounter between human and nonhuman life even less adequately than an epitaph for a human being can recall the person it commemorates.

In poem after poem, Hopkins expressed the fear that the rapid growth of the human population he saw around him in nineteenth-century Britain was cutting humankind off from forms of self-understanding that are only enabled by such contact with other kinds of life as "Binsey Poplars" records. In "The Sea and the Skylark," bird and ocean still have the power to shame the "sordid turbid time," but human beings can scarcely see or hear them any more, because they have fenced themselves in so thoroughly with the works of their own hands. As a result, Hopkins claims, "We, life's pride and cared-for crown,| Have lost that cheer and charm of earth's past prime" (29). Depression is not, however, the most lamentable consequence for humankind of its destruction of the remnants of Eden. For by destroying those pieces of the world in which, because they are wild, the original beauty of God's Creation can still be discerned, human beings prevent themselves from understanding their own proper role in it. This conviction is the origin of the fear, in "God's Grandeur," that the perpetually accumulating signs of human labor, which leave the world "smeared with trade; bleared with toil," are a crisis for Christian life. And it is behind the praise of wilderness in "Inversnaid" and "Ribblesdale," with its concise statement of human vocation: "What is Earth's eye, tongue, or heart else, where| Else, but in dear and dogged man." Humanity finds itself in a vicious circle: the more of the earth it ruins, the less understanding it has of the heartfelt care it ought to show for Creation, and the less understanding it has of this care, the more of the earth it ruins.

The "Earth, sweet Earth" of "Ribblesdale" has "no tongue to plead," but its plea is nonetheless strong "with him who dealt, nay does now deal,| Thy lovely dale down thus" (51). If Earth is victim, and God judge, human beings can be both witness and advocate to one another instead of merely criminal: witness to the fact that other living things also have the capacity to develop into fully distinctive individuals and advocate of their right to do so when it is denied to them by reckless human encroachment. It is this thought that binds together the halves of the sonnet "As kingfishers catch fire, dragonflies draw flame":

As kingfishers catch fire, dragonflies draw flame;
As tumbled over rim in roundy wells
Stones ring; like each tucked string tells, each hung bell's
Bow swung finds tongue to fling out broad its name;
Each mortal thing does one thing and the same:
Deals out that being indoors each one dwells;
Selves—goes itself; *myself* it speaks and spells,
Crying *Whát I dó is me: for that I came.* (51)

The invented verb "selves" once again makes the claim that the forms of self-realization witnessed in nonhuman lives are as individual and specific as human personhood.[21] Observation of nonhuman life in the octet turns to the formulation of its consequences for human ethics in the sestet. As in "Binsey Poplars," a break between the two parts of the poem mimes the ethical revelation that emerges from the experience of instress: "I say móre: the just man justices; | Keeps gráce: thát keeps all his goings graces." "Móre," "gráce," "thát": Hopkins's idiosyncratic accentual system hammers home his belief that right observation entails right action as insistently as the repetition that ends "Binsey Poplars."

How, then, is careful observation of the self-expressive activity of kingfishers and dragonflies related to the justice that makes a human being graceful? The just man, Hopkins tells us, "Acts in God's eye what in God's eye he is— | Chríst." As a human observer can see and celebrate how every animal is filled with the same drive to selfhood that animates his own being, so God looks at human beings and is delighted to witness the emergence of his own Christhood in them: "Christ plays in ten thousand places, | Lovely in limbs, and lovely in eyes not his." Humankind's endeavor to be "Earth's eye, tongue, or heart"—a witness and advocate for particularities of selfhood analogous to its own in other forms of life—emulates the activity of God, Who contemplates with enjoyment the evidence of his own incarnation in human beings.

Hopkins's feeling for the particularities of inscape as they manifest themselves in different animals of the same species can be gauged by comparing "The Sea and the Skylark" (29) with "The Caged Skylark" (31). While the bird of the first poem challenges human achievement with his "rash-fresh re-

21. Day (2004) notes the poem's kinship to "Binsey Poplars" in this respect and usefully compares Hopkins's concern for the particularities of nonhuman life in these poems with those of contemporary ecological writing.

winded new-skeinèd score," the second, "scanted in a dull cage," more closely matches the poet's own condition. Both bird and poet live lives of drudgery, "day-laboring-out life's age," for both are denied the alternation between satisfying, self-expressive exertion and pleasant repose that the bird would have if it were in its own nest, and not a man-made prison. Both, therefore, resemble the angry day laborers of "Tom's Garland" (64) denied the opportunity to do satisfying work by being set to the task of disfiguring the earth by employers who profit from their alienated labor.

One way, then, Hopkins thought, to imagine what satisfying human labor would look and feel like is to observe what animals do when left to their own devices. This is the same conclusion that Ezra Pound came to in his cage at Pisa. One critic has described the Pisan *Cantos* as a twentieth-century *Walden*:[22] Pound's confinement more or less obliged him to engage in the kind of close study of the natural world he had always admired but seldom undertaken himself for any extended period of time.[23] For at Pisa, Pound had little opportunity to do anything else but pay attention to what he could see, and among the things he could see were ants and wasps. As time went by, he came to look at them ever more observantly.

At the beginning of the Pisan *Cantos*, Pound discovers his own catastrophe in a solitary ant: "As a lone ant from a broken ant-hill | from the wreckage of Europe, ego scriptor" (*Canto* LXXVI, 478).[24] The identification is poignant, but somewhat narcissistic: it tells us a great deal about how the poet is feeling, but not much about the ant, who is avowedly metaphorical. As the sequence continues, however, the scriptor begins to pay more attention to what the insects around him are doing for themselves, and to draw lessons from it about his errors, rather than merely using them to illustrate his suffering. When, in *Canto* LXXXIII, he observes Brother Wasp "building a very neat house | of four rooms," or Madame La Vespa, who "in about 1/2 a day . . . has made her adobe," the "tiny mud-flask" that each of them constructs for their young is of a piece with human building at its best. The revelation that the most exquisite art may appear in the service of others comes as a shock to the poet and brings his own work to a halt: "and that day I wrote no further" (552–53).

22. Bush 1999, 115.

23. Cf. I. F. A. Bell on Pound's admiration for the biologist Louis Agassiz, whose injunction to his students that they practice "intelligent seeing," supplies the critical method of the *ABC of Reading*: "Look, look, look" (1981, 103–19).

24. Pound (1996, 478). All cantos cited in the text are from this edition.

The wasps of the Pisan *Cantos* are not mere symbols, animals put to use to express human capabilities or achievements. Rather, they allow Pound to reintegrate the artistry of human labor, his own included, into the biosphere, so that he can declare: "it is not man | Made courage, or made order, or made grace" (LXXXI, 541).[25] To "Learn of the green world what can be thy place | In scaled invention or true artistry" requires, first of all, simply paying attention, but with attention comes an understanding that human cultural activity is most effective when it is in harmony with forms of nonhuman activity that need not be posited as conscious goals by their agents (LXXXIII, 551):

> And now the ants seem to stagger
> > as the dawn sun has trapped their shadows,
> this breath wholly covers the mountains
> > it shines and divides
> it nourishes by its rectitude
> does no injury
> overstanding the earth it fills the nine fields
> > to heaven

Pound epitomizes the sage's understanding of what it is to "move with the seed's breath" in the words of a Venetian servant he had known—"non combaattere"—which he glosses as "don't work so hard," and he illustrates her saying with the ideograms "not," "help," and "grow" from Mencius's story of Kung-Sun Chow, a farmer who tried to get his crops to grow more quickly by pulling on them.[26] The ideogrammatic injunction helps us grasp Pound's claim, at the end of the *Cantos* as a whole, that "two mice and a moth" have been his guides in formulating its final protreptic: "To be men not destroyers"

25. Contemporary biology has found a similar voice in Margulis, who claims, "we did not 'invent' agriculture or locomotion on horseback, we became involved in the life cycles of plants and animals" (1986, 195), and, with respect to architecture, in particular, that "next to hundreds of cubic kilometers of tropical reefs built by coral and entire cliffs of chalk precipitated by foraminifera and coccolithophorids, human technology does not seem uniquely grand" (Margulis and Sagan 1995, 238). Cf. Ingold (1988, 86–90) on Lewis Henry Morgan's account of the engineering work of the beaver and the sense of commonality with human purposiveness it gave him.

26. Terrell (1984, 2:461). Lan helpfully reveals how Pound fashioned "a sort of eco-ethical discourse rare in its time" (2005, 168) from his creative engagement with the Confucian classics, and Mencius in particular. His detailed study of Pound's Chinese sources is a valuable complement to the fine readings of this passage in Read (1957, 405) and Bush (1999, 115–16).

(Notes for CXVII et seq., 823).[27] Human culture becomes humane through attention to the nonhuman, and, like Hopkins, Pound illustrates his conviction with a comparison between the work of larks and men:

La faillite de François Bernouard, Paris
or a field of larks at Allègre,
        "es laissa cader"
so high toward the sun and then falling,
        "de joi sas alas"
to set here the roads of France

The rise and fall of the publisher François Bernouard is contrasted with the flight of Bernart de Ventadorn's larks, who rise and fall on "wings of joy." The interleafing of the two is the simplest compositional device imaginable, and much of its effect depends upon the juxtaposition of place names at line end: "La faillite de François Bernouard, Paris" has the anonymity of a civic notice, Allègre gets its full semantic weight from the larks' joy. A modern metropolis that failed its writers is contrasted with a medieval city that honored them. By naming itself after the joy of the birds with whom it shared its place, Allègre showed itself to have rightly understood the relationship between the creativity of human beings and the characteristic self-expression of other animals. It is why Pound looks back to it as a model for his own labor, "to set here the roads of France."

WHAT POEMS KNOW

For Pound, to be men not destroyers means, as it does for Hopkins, to be "Earth's eye, tongue, or heart." Seeing and cherishing the kind of work that has made the nonhuman world what it is brings comprehension of the kind of work poets are called upon to do. Hopkins's lifelong experiments with rhythm were aimed at developing metrical resources flexible enough to communicate the living energies of inscape in all of its varieties. The thinning out of the page in the later *Cantos*—the sparse layout and short lines that let gnomic thats and infinitives float free in their zones of impersonal persuasion—reflects a trust in instances of right observation without the need for system,

---

27. Taylor (1999, 186) discusses the editorial questions surrounding the end of the poem and concludes that this passage is in fact the ending that Pound intended and authorized.

as Pound attuned his verse to the lapidary force of the Confucian records, whose writers "left blanks (for what they didn't know)."[28]

Both poets, at moments in their careers, explained their distinctive practice with reference to their dissatisfaction with Walt Whitman. Hopkins, in a letter to Robert Bridges, explained that Whitman's mind was more like his own "than any man's living," but that the "last ruggedness and decomposition into common prose" of Whitman's verse was in the end inferior to the "last elaboration" of meter in his own, because Whitman's exclusive dedication to the task of self-expression curtailed any corresponding disclosure of others.[29] For Pound, Whitman's genius was a willing identification with "his function" for "his time and his people."[30]

For both Hopkins and Pound, their great predecessor suffers from a kind of deliberate self-limitation: to the perfection of self-image in Hopkins's view, to a vatic persona standing for the will of a historical group in Pound's. For both poets, a remedy was discovered in turning outward, in the "intelligent seeing" that enables trans-species and hence trans-historical understanding. Dragonflies and kingfishers allow Hopkins access to the eyes of God; ants and wasps allow Pound access to the mind of the Confucian sage. Biophilia enables alternatives to Whitman's way of being in the world that, for all its expansive articulation, is a foreclosure of human possibilities. In the remainder of this chapter, I want to attempt some broader theorization of the modes of understanding the lyric practice of Hopkins and Pound offers us.

I began this chapter with narrative texts by Flaubert and Milton, and I used an Aristotelian concept of *mythos* to recoup from them a species level reflection on human behavior. While Aristotle is less explicit than he might be about "the epistemological assumptions of his inquiry into the art of poetry,"[31] his argument in the *Poetics* that fictional narratives instantiate general truths of human behavior is continuous with his understanding that the human being is one kind of political animal among others:[32] it is because generalities of social behavior can be discerned in humankind as a whole that the focused distillation of such behavior in the plots of narrative poems can make these generalities apparent to readers.

28. Pound 1947, 267.
29. Letter to Robert Bridges of October 18, 1882; Hopkins 1991, 170–73.
30. "What I Feel about Walt Whitman," in Pound (1975, 145).
31. Doležel 1990, 16.
32. I will discuss this connection in more detail in the following chapters.

Aristotle never claims that poets arrive at their plots through observation, as scientists arrive at their conclusions about the behavior of other animals. They do not know what their fictions contain in a way that they could state in propositional form. Rather, audiences and readers actualize the latent descriptive viability of narrative fictions as they take their emotional response to them as an index of their verisimilitude. Aristotle sidesteps Socrates' efforts, in a number of Platonic dialogues, to identify what poems know with what poets know by showing the irrelevance of this endeavor for the modes of understanding proper to narrative fiction. But what of lyric poetry? If particular poems articulate a transformed understanding of human being that does proceed from direct observation of other forms of life, can these claims become a general account of a different mode of *poiesis*? Is it desirable that they should?

I suggest that the answers to these questions are yes they can, and, yes they should. Let me begin with Martin Heidegger's rejection of fictionality as the ground of poetic truth in the "Letter on Humanism." Here Heidegger claims that "Aristotle's words, although they have scarcely been pondered, are still valid—that poetic composition is truer than exploration of beings [das Erkunden von Seienden]."[33] Heidegger translates Aristotle's *historia*, usually rendered "history" in this passage (*Poetics* 9, 1451b5), as "exploration of beings," using a phrase for the single Greek word that brings out the wide range of its original referents: both Herodotus's *History* and Aristotle's *History of Animals* are examples of *historia*. Heidegger's translation also brings out the degree to which Greek *historia*, as exploration of beings, involves direct observation. *Historia* is the kind of first person autopsy that provides matter for further reflection, one form of the latter being *poiesis*, and another philosophy.[34] It is this subsequent dwelling in thought with what has been observed, that, on any translation, makes *poiesis* a more serious and philosophical endeavor than *historia*, although the nature of the secondary labor that distinguishes poetry from philosophy has still to be identified.

In "What Are Poets For?" Heidegger glosses this movement from first person observation to poetic reflection as a progress from "the work of the eyes"

33. Heidegger (1977b, 264). Cf. Heidegger (1971, 72): "Poetry . . . is not an aimless imagining of whimsicalities and not a flight of mere notions into the realm of the unreal."

34. For example, the kind of philosophical reflection undertaken by Aristotle in the zoological works that follow the *History of Animals* (the *Parts of Animals*, *Movement of Animals*, and *Progression of Animals*) and which moves beyond observation in an effort to understand the significance of what has been observed; see Preus (1975, 1).

to "the work of the heart."[35] Because poetry eschews the "covetous vision of things" that is present in technological understanding, and "does not solicit anything to be produced" in its encounters with other living things, it enables humankind to apprehend itself as one kind of being among others, and so offers it an adumbration of Being that philosophy labors in its own way to articulate. Heidegger's claim emerges from a discussion of a verse of Rilke— "Only the song's high breath | hallows and hails"—and it is easy enough to fault both for offering a version of the naming of animals in which other living things, like Lévinas's dog, have no power to compel recognition, and it is only the framing activity of human culture that allows them to be seen for what they are.[36] If, however, Heidegger's account of lyric poetry involves the "onto-theological determination" of difference Derrida has observed elsewhere in his philosophy,[37] his claim that the "painstaking cultivation" and "thorough craftsmanship" by which poets turn *historia* into *poiesis* must be understood as "work of the heart" points to what critical theory has had, essentially, to deprive itself of in its response to this determination.

Consider Whitman's "Song of the Redwood-Tree." The poet imagines that California redwoods rejoice in "the music of choppers' axes" as they are converted into lumber for "the new society at last proportionate to Nature"[38] Lower nature voluntarily offers itself to higher, because the higher understands the lower better than it understands itself. The poem has all the limitations identified by Hopkins and Pound, and its mode of false consciousness is as old as the *Homeric Hymn to Hermes*, in which the infant god imagines that a tortoise will be pleased to be turned into a lyre that human beings will play at feasts (l. 30–38).[39]

35. Heidegger 1971, 138.

36. Cf. the claim in Heidegger (1971, 42) that in the plastic arts, "tree and grass, eagle and bull, snake and cricket first enter into their distinctive shapes and thus come to appear as what they are" (1971, 42). How is one to distinguish such cultural work from the "stock-breeding and exploitation" discussed in Heidegger (1971, 112), in which perception of the good qualities of other living things precedes the "technical objectivation" that renders them more useful— more truly themselves—than they would have been otherwise?

37. Derrida (1991, 116). Cf. Calarco (2004) and Elden (2006) on the centrality of Heidegger's version of human exceptionalism to the discussion of human difference in the ethical thought of Lévinas and Derrida.

38. W. Whitman 1996, 353.

39. The most absurd enactment of this tradition of bad faith may be the "comedy of innocence" in Greek sacrificial cult: human beings induce a movement of the animal's head that is "understood" by participants in the ceremony to be a gesture of assent on the animal's part; see

It is one thing, however, to criticize the thinking that underwrites such paeans to destructivism; it is another thing entirely to engage in the heart work that might alter it. For this, as both Heidegger and Derrida suggest, we must look to other poets. So when Allen Ginsberg discovers Whitman wandering the meat aisle of "A Supermarket in California," hailing the late night shoppers `with uninvited questions, he thinks of taking him outside for a stroll through the "solitary streets." There they will contemplate together "the lost America of love," until Whitman can answer with sincerity a question addressed to him:

> what America did you have when Charon quit poling his ferry and
> you got out on a smoking bank and stood watching the boat
> disappear on the black waters of Lethe?[40]

Ginsberg calls Whitman a "lonely old courage-teacher," but suggests that the nexus of loneliness and courage in his poetry is the expression of a missed opportunity, an accommodation to an America that might have been otherwise. The suggestion is not an accusation, and the poem waits patiently for an answer that can never come. But Ginsberg imagines his unabashed affection leading Whitman back through the obfuscations of his work, so that he might rethink the America it in some sense enabled or excused. So Flaubert acknowledged that George Sand's friendship had provoked in him a desire to work "sincerely and from the heart" whose outcome was *Trois contes*.[41] For Flaubert was the last to believe that there was nothing better in the world than his own kind and he was glad to have found a reader who understood that his work was not a projection of the narcissism of his peers.

Burkert (1983, 4–5 and passim). Thoreau knew better. Reflecting, in *The Maine Woods*, on the "murder of the moose" he has just witnessed, he contrasts the work of the poet, who "makes the truest use" of "men and moose and pine-trees," because he knows their hearts without destroying them, with the work that goes on in "the lumber-yard, and the carpenter's shop, and the tannery, and the lamblack-factory, and the turpentine clearing" (Thoreau 1985, 685).

40. Ginsberg 2006, 144.
41. In letters to Edma Roger des Genettes, Flaubert (1997, 399–407).

PART TWO

Becoming Something Else

CHAPTER THREE

Beyond the Pale

*Joining the Society of Animals in Aristophanes, Herman Melville,
and Louis-Ferdinand Céline*

*The language of birds is very ancient, and, like other ancient modes of speech,
very elliptical: little is said, but much is meant and understood.*
—Gilbert White, *The Natural History of Selborne*, Letter XLIII

In the first half of this book, I explored the imaginative identification with
other animals enabled by aggression and the narcissistic aversion from them
manifested as destructiveness. In the second, I explore the attraction to the
society of other animals that finds expression in stories about human beings
who try to join them and the affects that cluster around the possibility that
the human body is susceptible in various ways to becoming animal. In this
chapter, then, I consider a number of narrative texts that engage our understanding that animals other than human beings live in social groups and communicate with one another as members of them: Aristophanes' *Birds*, Herman Melville's *Moby-Dick*, and Louis-Ferdinand Céline's *Rigadoon*. Each of
them exhibits a similar story pattern: a human being in exile from his society
gets firsthand experience of an animal society that exists alongside it, but par-
ticipation in the alternative forms of sociality these animal societies offer is in
the end denied to this outsider, who ends up more or less where he began, in
splendid or abject isolation. These thwarted attempts at forms of becoming
other willed by human subjects thus form a prelude to the kinds of unwilled
transformation that I examine in the metamorphosis narratives of my final
chapter.

ARISTOTLE'S BIRDS

Before considering Aristophanes' version of the animal society story pattern in *Birds*, I want to briefly consider Aristotle's position on the nature of human and animal societies as a kind of counterpoint to the playwright's imaginative engagement with the topic. Aristotle's account of human society in the *Politics* views its achievements against the horizon of zoological life as a whole, and his famous assertion that the human being is "by nature a political animal" is best understood by comparing his account of what is distinctive about human society with his descriptions of the kinds of sociality exhibited by other animals.

In the *History of Animals*, Aristotle asserts that there are other animals that are political in addition to human beings—his examples are bees, wasps, ants, and cranes—since among them too "one activity is common to all" (1.1, 488a8–9). He differentiates these animals from those that are merely gregarious, such as cows and fish, for while the latter live together in large groups, all the members of the group do the same thing at the same time. Political animals, by contrast, exhibit division of labor so that the common goals of the group to which they belong may be advanced more effectively. And, because groups can organize themselves in different ways so as to allow for division of labor, differences in political organization exist among the other political animals, just as they do among human beings: cranes and bees live under a single ruler, for example, whereas ants and many others get along without one.

As Aristotle sees it, the reason that the social formations of other political animals have not attained the degree of organization and specialization exhibited by human beings is that their means of communicating with one are too rudimentary to allow further development. Human beings possess reasoning speech (λόγος), whereas the other animals have only voice (φωνή). They can signify their sensations of pleasure and pain to one another, but only reasoning speech can make clear what is beneficial and harmful, and what is just and unjust, and so allow the ongoing elaboration of forms of sociality that are consciously developed by those who participate in them. It is with reasoning speech, Aristotle argues, that human beings advanced from the forms of social behavior exhibited by other animals to the household and then the city (*Politics* 1.2, 1253a1–18).[1]

---

1. For discussion of the naturalness of human social formations in the context of Aristotle's biological works and the importance of language within them, see Ambler (1985), Kullman

Given its importance in the zoological grounding of his political thought, it is not surprising that Aristotle offers a detailed account of the difference between human speech and the utterance of other animals in his biological works. He differentiates between sound (ψόφος), voice (φωνή), and articulate utterance (διάλεκτος), and claims that the ability to produce each of them depends upon the possession of particular somatic features. So while crustaceans and most kinds of fish are silent, some insects, like the cicada, are able to make a sound by moving parts of their bodies. Likewise, while frogs, dolphins, and most viviparous animals are able to emit a voice, because they have lungs and a windpipe, they do not have a fully flexible tongue and so are incapable of articulate utterance.

By "articulate utterance," Aristotle means a sequence of individualized sounds that have been divided by the action of a flexible tongue, and which differs as such from the roar of a lion or the trumpeting of an elephant, which are indivisible vocal emissions. Apart from human beings, only certain kinds of birds have a tongue capable of such division, and they are therefore the only other animals capable of articulate utterance, although they produce less of it than human beings do (*History of Animals* 2.12, 504b1–3, 4.9, 535a28–536a22).[2] As an observable phenomenon, the articulate utterance of birds resembles that of human beings in a number of ways: it shows regional variation, like the dialects of human speech, and in some kinds of birds its elements are demonstrably learned and not innate (536b11–18).[3] What remains cryptic, however, is what birds do with their articulate utterance; to what extent is their use of it is analogous to human conversation?

(1991), Depew (1995), and Cooper (2005). Arnhart (1994) has some surprising examples of how Aristotle's ideas about the social life of animals, and particularly insects, have been borne out by modern biology.

2. My understanding of Aristotle's biology of language is indebted to Zirin (1980), the main lines of which I follow here. Aristotle's claim at 536a1, that human beings alone possess διάλεκτος, would seem to contradict not only the assertion at 504b1, that certain kinds of birds, because of their flexible tongues, are second only to human beings in giving voice to γράμματα, but also the equally explicit assertion at 536a20 that broad-tongued birds produce articulate utterance, διάλεκτον. The best explanation of the apparent contradiction would seem to be that at 536a1 διάλεκτος is employed, somewhat confusingly, as a synonym for λόγος, in anticipation of the discussion of human language acquisition that follows.

3. Cf. Kroodsma (2005, 15, 42, 87, 141, 150), on innate versus learned birdsong, with explicit comparison to human language acquisition, and discussion of the role of learned song repertories in avian social networks. A CD accompanying this book helps readers identify the articulation of sonic units in the birdsongs he discusses.

In the *Politics*, Aristotle claims that the voice of animals is merely a sign: they can indicate their affective states to one another with it but cannot discuss their causes. This position is consistent with the biological works, where we are told that male frogs, for example, call upon females with their croak at breeding time, and that all animals possessing a voice use it to produce distinctive sounds for the purposes of association and sexual intercourse (536a9–16). In these animals, the voice is merely a signal that contains a single item of information at a time. They emit a specific sound in response to a specific affective event, and, in doing so, they are seeking a specific behavior on the part of its recipient (the sound may of course be repeated until this outcome is achieved).

Birds, on the other hand, have more than voice, and there is therefore room for doubt about what their articulate utterance enacts, and especially whether, like the articulate utterance of human beings, it is reciprocal and so amounts to a genuine conversational exchange. Aristotle hints at this possibility in the *History of Animals*. In his discussion of local variation, he claims that the articulate utterance of birds is a capacity that "one might call a kind of speech" [ἣν ἄν τις ὥσπερ διάλεκτον εἴπειεν] (536b9–13). A passage from the *Parts of Animals* reiterates the claim more forcefully:

> All birds make use of their tongue to communicate with one another [πρὸς ἑρμηνείαν ἀλλήλοις], and some very much more so than others, so that with some there does indeed seem to be an exchange of knowledge among them [ὥστ᾽ ἐπ᾽ ἐνίων καὶ μάθησιν εἶναι δοκεῖν παρ᾽ ἀλλήλων]. (2.17, 660a35–b3)

Aristotle concludes the passage with a reference to the earlier work, and it looks very much as if he intended to give a definitive answer here to the question raised by his first treatment of the topic by asserting a closer approximation to human speech in the articulate utterance of birds than he had previously been willing to allow.

When considered in terms of its physiological production, its material constitution, its learned acquisition, and its apparent social function, the articulate utterance of birds cannot be distinguished from that of human beings. In order to do so, nonobservable features have to be invoked. In the *Nicomachean Ethics*, Aristotle claims that mind (νοῦς) is the contemplative faculty that separates human beings from all other animals, and allows them to approach the divine (10.7.8, 1177b27–78a2). Mind is incorporeal, but its presence in human speech must be understood if human speech is to be distinguished from the utterance of birds. The biological works are unable to make this distinction on the basis of observation alone.[4]

Suppose, however, that we were not to take the escape route offered by incorporeal minds and stick to observable phenomena instead. Where would this path take us if we were to pursue it further? It is a fundamental principle of Aristotle's zoology that animals' distinctive bodies are realizations of their distinctive natures.[5] It is in the *Parts of Animals, Movement of Animals*, and *Progression of Animals* that this philosophical claim meets biological reality "head-on," as these works offer reasons for the variety of animal bodies documented in the *History of Animals*.[6] So, for example, while the *History of Animals* catalogues the variety of birds' feet, the *Parts of Animals* argues that this variety allows each kind of bird to pursue the life appropriate to it (694b6, 648a16). If certain kinds of birds have a distinctive kind of tongue, then, and they use this tongue to produce articulate utterance similar to that of human beings, we ought to ask how this tongue and the utterance it enables contribute to their realization of a distinctive way of life. In particular, if speech is what has allowed human beings to realize their distinctive forms of political society, it seems obvious to wonder what forms of sociality have been enabled by the articulate utterance of birds, and whether they resemble the forms of human society as closely as the two forms of articulate utterance resemble one another.

For Aristotle, the problem with birds is that extensive observation of their social lives is considerably more difficult than such observation of the smaller political animals. Aristotle's willingness to cite the testimony of those who worked closely with animals in their professional lives—beekeepers, fishermen, eel farmers, and the like—has frequently been remarked.[7] In both accounts of bird utterance, however, he emphasizes what is suggested to the mind by autopsy of wild birds but has not been confirmed by continuous observation: "the articulated voice of birds, *which one might call a kind of speech*, differs in various animals and also within the same kind of animal

4. Zirin (1980 345–46); Kullmann (1991, 115). So too, in *On the Soul*, Aristotle asserts that νοῦς is not present until the activity of thinking begins, that it is not mixed with the body, and that, unlike the faculty of perception, it has no organ (3.4, 429a22–27). It is on this basis that Lennox (1999) argues that, for Aristotle, there are definite limits to a zoological account of human beings.

5. "Nature makes nothing without purpose or in vain," as it is formulated in the *Politics* (1.3.7, 1256b21); for discussion, see Preus (1975, 1–13); G. E. R. Lloyd (1991, 46–56); French (1994, 178); Depew (1995, 164).

6. Preus 1975, 1.

7. Preus 1975, 36; G. E. R. Lloyd 1987, 53.

according to location"; "all birds make use of their tongue in order to communicate with one another, and some very much more so than others, so that
in certain ones *there does indeed seem to be an exchange of knowledge among
them.*" In both passages, Aristotle contrasts observation with what can legiti-
mately be concluded from observation, and, as he does so, acknowledges the
way in which one is tempted, on the basis of observation, to go beyond what
can be truly known from it. When you see birds singing, you cannot help but
think they are talking to one another; that's just how it looks.[8]

ARISTOPHANES' *BIRDS*

Aristotle's acknowledgment of the directions an observer might take in
expanding on the way things look is an understated announcement of how
imagination enters the scene of observation. From this place of natural wonder, one path leads to hypothesis, verification, and falsifiability, and another
to literary fantasy, in which the ordinary observer's instinctive flights of fancy
about the lives of other animals become a fully fledged imaginative reality.
Such fantasies are at the heart of the subgenre of Old Comedy to which Aristophanes' *Birds* belongs: plays like *Goats*, *Wild Animals*, and *Fish* stage het-
erotopian encounters between human beings and other animals in which
these animals voice their own understanding of their lives and the ways in
which they have been hijacked by the human culture that makes use of them
for food and labor.[9]

Aristophanes' *Birds* belongs to this comic tradition, but it suspends any
easy understanding of how the site of its comic fantasy is positioned in relationship to everyday reality. Normally, the first action of the first character

8. On the parrot, a favorite topic of subsequent discussions of animal language in antiquity, see Sorabji (1993, 80–81). A single captive bird is, however, of little value in ascertaining
whether groups of birds of the same species converse with one another in the wild.

9. On fantasy as the "primary mode" of Aristophanic comedy, to which "satire and critical
observation are foils," see C. Whitman (1964, 7–16). Wilkins (2000a, 349) describes how Old
Comedy combined the animal choruses it inherited from earlier forms of ritual performance
with a critical attention to eating practices in city life to produce dramas in which animals'
vocal objections to being eaten loom large. Wilkins (2000b, 23–25) discusses this theme in
Aristophanes' *Birds*. As Wilkins (2000a, 348) points out, Crates's *Wild Animals* seems to imi-
tate a fragment of Empedocles on vegetarian diet (31 B141 DK), and the comic playwrights as
a whole seem to have been aware of philosophical treatments of the relations between human
beings and other animals. The prehistory of the animal choruses of Old Comedy is discussed
by Sifakis (1971, 76–85), and Rothwell (2007, 6–36), who also considers *Birds* as a parody of
philosophical accounts of the emergence of human society from savagery (151–82).

to appear on an ancient stage is to state his name, place, and business, and so allow the audience to grasp the fictional situation.[10] Instead, the heroes of *Birds*, Peisetairus and Euelpides, wander back and forth on stage with a jackdaw and a crow that are supposed to be their guides, but whose instructions they are unable to understand. They have no idea where the rocky wilderness in which they are wandering is located, or if they can find their way back home again from it (11–12). The declaration of no-topia is followed by a list of reasons why Athens no longer feels like home: illegal immigrants, interminable legal procedures, and endless foreign wars (27–48). Athens itself is as imaginary as the place in which they are to be imagined.

Peisetairus's hopes for a better life rest on his plan to find Tereus, the tragic hero who was turned into a hoopoe for his crimes against humanity and who now haunts the empty spaces between human habitations. Peisetairus hopes that Tereus may have spotted in his travels a city where he and his companion might live with minimal interference from other people. From an ornithological perspective, however, Peisetairus is himself the hoopoe that he seeks. Aristotle, in his discussion of the lifestyles of birds in the *History of Animals*, cites a long passage he claims is from Aeschylus, in which the hoopoe (ἔποψ) is described as "the overseer [ἐπόπτης] of his own evils." Aeschylus describes the bird as a shape shifter that leaves its spring haunts full of hatred, and "sets off to relocate [ἀποικίσει] in deserted woods and cliffs."[11] As Aeschylus tells it, Tereus, transformed into a hoopoe after the grisly events at home, haunts the margins of human society as an exile from it, drawn back periodically, but unable to stomach it for long. He no longer loathes just his own family but all human beings, and has become a perpetual colonist, forever striking out in search of *terra incognita*.[12]

The behavior of the hoopoe is the common denominator of a way of life both Tereus and Peisetairus instantiate, and we wonder how two such misanthropic beings will be able to share the stage as the moment of their encounter approaches. The crow and the jackdaw having been trying to point out something to their handlers for some time, and at last they get their message across: the stage building still has a door in it even though it represents a rock, and Euelpides bangs on it to summon the birds on the other side. As he does so,

10. See Payne (2007, 51–53) on creative experimentation with this convention in later comedy.

11. Aeschylus frag. 304, at *HA* 633a19–28.

12. Cf. Forbes Irving (1990, 233–60) on avian metamorphosis as a special class of story in which transformed human beings do not turn back into what they were but exhibit characteristic traits of their prior selves as the bird they have become.

he shouts "Boy, boy" [παῖ, παῖ], as if he were calling a house slave to answer the door, but Peisetairus suggests that when summoning a hoopoe (ἔποπα) one ought rather to shout "oh hoopoe" [ἐποποῖ] (56–60), a sound that is both a vocative of the noun "hoopoe" and a curtailed version of the nonverbal exclamations of a tragic hero in pain, which is, of course, what Tereus had been before his transformation into a bird.

The outbursts of pain in Sophocles' *Philoctetes* are the most extensive examples of such utterance by tragic heroes, for in this play they extend to half lines and even, on one occasion, to a whole line of verse: ἀπαππαπαῖ, παπᾶ παπᾶ παπᾶ παπαῖ (746). Philoctetes' cries are an indication of his suffering, much as the φωνή of nonhuman animals is—so Aristotle claims—a sign of their affective condition without being language as such (*Politics* 1.1.10, 1253a11–13). And so it is that these nonverbal utterances drive away other human beings and cut Philoctetes off from human society: as H. P. Lovecraft observes in "The Call of Cthulhu," "there are vocal qualities peculiar to men, and vocal qualities peculiar to beasts; and it is terrible to hear the one when the source should yield the other."[13]

In *Birds*, however, the human characters' adoption of a form of utterance that mixes articulate speech with nonverbal indication is a literal "open sesame." In the opening lines of the play, Peisetairus and Euelpides respond to their inability to grasp the exact import of the croaking of the crow and jackdaw with frustration: Peisetarus's suggestion that Euelpides make a noise (ψόφος) to attract attention by hitting his head with a rock (55) is a reversion to the most primitive form of animal sound production imagined by Aristotle, namely, striking one body part against another, or against an inanimate object. The vocalization ἐποποῖ, on the other hand, works wonders; it rolls back the door of Tereus's kingdom (the inhabitants of which have hitherto remained deaf to the banging) and overcomes the gulf between human speech and animal indication for the duration of the play. Like birds whose songs are acquired rather than innate, Peisetairus and Euelpides must learn new sounds to enter a new territory.[14]

Puns typically find humor in a surprising coincidence of sound in two words with different meanings. Here, however, one of the components of the pun is not a word at all, but merely a sequence of sounds that functions as a signal of affect in a particular cultural discourse. The "pun" heralds the investigation of continuities between human speech and bird song later in the play,

13. Lovecraft 2005, 179.
14. Cf. Kroodsma 2005, 55.

but also points to the bestialization of tragic heroes who lose the power of reasoning speech because of the intensity of their feeling. In this respect, it is continuous with what happens when the hoopoe's house slave does finally open the door: Peisetairus and Euelpides are so afraid that they soil themselves. For here, the typically comic manifestation of fear does not simply point to an awkward fact of human physiology, it also turns Peisetairus and Euelpides into birds: one becomes a "fearbelow, a Libyan bird," the other a "shat-on, from Phasis."

Once the heroes' continuity with bird life has been established, they are able to approach the doorman on equal terms. Peisetairus asks him, "What kind of bird are you?" and, when the doorman replies that he is a "slave bird," Peisetairus assumes he must have lost to a superior bird in a cockfight, resulting in his enslavement (65–71). The set of resemblances between human beings and birds embraces their affective responses, the bodily functions these affects induce, and the social structures in which weakness and strength are encoded as the submission of the servile to the noble.[15] This looks like a workable basis for mutual understanding, and the crow and jackdaw disappear now that these symmetries between human and bird societies have been established.

Peisetairus calls Euelpides "a cowardly beast" [θηρίον] for being afraid of the doorman (87–88), and, when Tereus makes his appearance a few lines later, he exclaims, "What beast [θηρίον], is this?" (92). Continuities between human and nonhuman life are asserted clearly enough in lines such as these, but how are they instantiated on stage? *Birds* is one of only two comedies we know of in which the chorus members were individually costumed: in this play they represent different kinds of birds, in the *Cities* of Eupolis they represented specific cities.[16] The actors, however, comment upon their own lackluster appearance in typical comic fashion. When Peisetairus notes Tereus's feathers and triple crest, Euelpides remarks that, "the twelve gods seem to have messed you up." Tereus's costume is shabby and disheveled, and Peisetairus and Euelpides later complain that their transformation into birds is just as poorly represented (802–8).[17]

Perhaps we should imagine a contrast between the half-hearted portrayal of

15. For a study of the Greek cockfight as an enactment of anxieties about the relationship between sexual and social submission, see Csapo (1993a, 1993b), who also discusses the controversial identification of men dressed as cocks on a vase painting as the *agon* of a comic play.

16. See Dunbar (1998, 167), who discusses the possibility that, in addition to the *Cities*, the *Konnos* of Ameipsias may have had a chorus of individually named philosophers.

17. See Romer 1983, Csapo 1993a, 4.

Peisetairus, Euelpides, and Tereus, who are transformed human beings, and the chorus, who are birds and nothing but birds. In any case, if comic actors often draw attention to the inadequacies of their costume in order to remind us of "another character beneath the incongruous disguise,"[18] this typical feature of the genre, like the others we have noted, has a special resonance in this play, because it focuses the audience's attention not upon one human being's ability to impersonate another more or less successfully, but upon the differences in physical appearance between two kinds of animal whose similarities of affect and social organization are explored thematically. The idea that human difference is immediately apparent in the human body is suspended.

Tereus gives two explanations for his wretched appearance: Sophocles made him look bad by giving him a beak in his tragedy, and his plumage is shabby because birds molt in winter (100–7). For Tereus, his metamorphosis is an imposition; he has to endure the body and life cycle of a bird as a punishment that originates in his tragic myth. Peisetairus, however, invokes nonobservable phenomena to revalue Tereus's transformation. He claims that, having lived as a human being and as a bird, Tereus can think "all that a human being thinks and all that a bird thinks" (117–19). For Peisetairus, Tereus is not an impaired human being but a double life-form. He is like the animals Aristotle calls "dualizers" because they participate in the lifestyle of two kinds of animal at once, as seals, for example, live partly as land animals and partly as sea animals.[19]

Peisetairus reimagines tragic bestialization as comic opportunity. The behavior of the hoopoe suggests a resemblance between Peisetairus and Tereus as human types, but Peisetairus moves beyond such local analogies by identifying Tereus as the common denominator between the lifestyles of human beings and birds as a whole. He now begins to formulate a plan that is quite different from the one with which he set out to look for Tereus. Instead of seeking a city in which he can live in peace, he will make a city of birds by transforming the loose social agglomeration in which they currently live from a mere place in the sky—a *polos*, as he calls it—to a city as such, a *polis* (179–86).

Peisetairus chooses as the model for his new city the form of social organization he knows best. Becoming a city means building fortifications, for fortifications will allow the birds to rule over human beings as they currently rule over insects and to starve the gods into submission by cutting off the flow of

18. Foley 2000, 305.
19. See Cooper (2005, 80–82n5) for a discussion of human beings as dualizers in their alternation between solitary and herding lifestyles.

sacrificial smoke, as the Athenians reduced the island of Melos by blockading it.[20] All that is required for this plan to succeed is the reduction of the multiple forms of avian sociality to a single form of human society, and, in the scenes that follow, the audience is given an extensive lyrical evocation of the diverse forms of bird life it is Peisetairus's intention to replace.

Tereus promises to summon the birds so that he can explain Peisetairus's plan to them, which he is able to do because he has taught them to understand the human voice (φωνή): birds are no longer barbarians requiring an interpreter to understand Greek (199–200). As Tereus calls them, he describes their varied habitats and feeding behaviors, from seed gatherers in sown fields and meadow-dwelling insect eaters to exotic oceanic kingfishers. He rounds out each summons with strings of syllables that weave together the articulate sounds of bird song with human words that resemble them. Vocalizations that start out as pure sound—*ito, ito, ito, ito, ito, ito* (ἴτω ἴτω ἴτω ἴτω ἴτω ἴτω), turn into its homophone, the imperative "come" (ἴτω), then revert to pure sound once again: *torotorotorotorotinx, kikkabow, kikkabow.*

As many commentators have noted, this song is the pinnacle of Aristophanes' achievement as a lyric poet and musician.[21] It is answered by the arrival of the chorus, who instantiate the diversity it describes. The birds arrive in silence, and remain silent in response to the clownish comments on their appearance by Peisetairus and Euelpides.[22] A variety of reasons for this silence might be imagined and actualized in performance: the birds' fear of, or hostility toward, the men who have intruded into their world; suspense as to whether they can talk, like their half-human summoner, or whether they will utter only the nonhuman sounds of which his song is partially made up; or contrast between the splendid portrayal of natural diversity and the inane human chatter with which it is greeted. In any case, twenty-eight kinds of bird eventually appear that show a wide spectrum of avian life, both domestic and foreign: flamingo, cockerel, another hoopoe, partridge, francolin, widgeon, kingfisher, owl, jay, turtle dove, lark, reed warbler, thyme finch, rock dove, vulture, hawk, ring dove, cuckoo, redshank, shrike, gallinule, kestrel, grebe, bunting, lammergeier, woodpecker.[23]

20. Cf. the classic commentary on *Birds* as a critique of Athenian imperial ambitions in Arrowsmith (1973).

21. Perkell 1993, 2; Daitz 1997, 314; Parker 1997, 297–302; Dunbar 1998, 155–58.

22. Dunbar 1998, 167.

23. I follow the identification in Dunbar (1998, 176–84) of the twenty-four birds that make up the chorus, plus the four additional birds that precede them, omitting the two she considers unidentifiable. These identifications are discussed in detail in Dunbar (1997, 124–29).

The play in fact contains a humorous reminder that this fulsome representation of avian diversity is in reality no more than a sample. After his foundation of the new city of Cloudcuckooland, Peisetairus has a priest perform an inaugural sacrifice to the bird gods that will preside over it. He begins by reassigning the functions of the Olympians to birds, and then offers a conventional prayer whose intention is to ensure that no god has been omitted from the list of those receiving sacrifice (867). This formula ought to end the ceremony,[24] but Peisetairus responds by hailing the "Hawk of Sunium," thereby setting the priest off on a new set of divinities. He begins with further bird and Olympian hybrids, gestures at a second closing formula with the mention of the Chians—Athenian allies who "creep in everywhere"—then launches into a seemingly interminable list of birds in a last ditch effort at sacral completeness: "The white pelican and the gray pelican and the marsh harrier and the sand grouse and the peacock and the reed warbler and the teal and the skua and the heron and the tern and the blackcap and the great tit . . ." (881–88).

Peisetairus truncates the priest's invocation in mid-catalogue, a reminder that the transference of customary formulas of religious inclusiveness to birds will take some time if their intention to honor each and every member of the divine kind is taken seriously. The invocation, like the chorus, is a parade of biodiversity in keeping with the celebration of material abundance in the work of Aristophanes and Old Comedy as a whole.[25] Birds, more than other animals, were the subjects of etiological stories that gave reasons for the abundant variety of their forms,[26] and it seems reasonable to conclude that they were the animals in which the variety of nonhuman bodies presented itself most forcefully as a source of wonder to inhabitants of the Attic peninsula.[27]

Tereus overcomes the birds' initial hostility to Peisetairus and Euelpides as human beings, and hence age-old hunters of their own kind (328, 369), by convincing them that, while men in general may be their enemies "by nature" [τὴν φύσιν], these particular men are friends by virtue of their minds (τὸν νοῦν). The slightly awkward contrast between "enemies by nature" and

24. Dunbar 1998, 346.
25. Cf. Storey (2003, 68) on the lines from Eupolis's *Goats* in which these animals rattle through twenty-four plants and trees on which they feed in five lines, and Wilkins (2000b, 1–51) on "Comedy and the material world."
26. Forbes Irving 1990, 96.
27. Although it should be added that the choice of birds as the most striking parallel to human diversity among the other animals is not a uniquely Greek phenomenon: both Farid ud-Din Attar's *Conference of Birds* and Chaucer's *Parliament of Fowls* choose birds to analogize the variety of humankind, and, in the former, the hoopoe is also the spiritual leader of the avian pilgrims.

"friends by mind" points to a double meaning in *nous*, which may be either the rational mind as such or the calculation of which it is capable. The men are not friends to the birds just because they have overcome their natural inclinations by thinking rationally but because they have a plan that involves them. The deliberative power that, for Aristotle, distinguishes human beings from other animals is identified here with the capacity to envisage others as instruments that can be made to serve one's own goals.

In his efforts to convince the birds that their present subjection to human power is a humiliation from which they can free themselves with his aid, Peisetairus treats them to a fearsome catalogue of bird trapping tools: nets, nooses, snares, traps, and birdlime (524–28). The list is both typically comic in its exhaustive approach to a particular area of material culture and grimly mimetic in its performance: it is the part of the comic drama called the *pnigos* ("choker"), an extended utterance delivered by the actor in a single breath. It is the kind of protest speech at human cruelty that, elsewhere in Old Comedy, is put into the mouths of the animals themselves,[28] and its content looks to be parodic of the so-called "Ode to Man" in Sophocles' *Antigone*, where the "nets of woven coils" in which human beings trap birds, beasts, and fish are one of the pieces of evidence adduced for the uncanny cunning they manifest in their mastery of the natural world (342–47). Peisetairus, whose name means persuasion, demonstrates his superiority to Sophoclean man by employing nets of words to entrap his less sophisticated interlocutors.

Generic expectations as to who will speak what are also suspended in the parabasis. Here, for the first time in Aristophanes' drama, the chorus remains in character; it addresses the audience as birds, voicing its own concerns, not those of the poet. What these talking birds have to say is none too flattering to their human listeners; they call them "feeble in natural life," "like the generation of leaves," "powerless," "things made of mud," "a strengthless race of shadow shapes," "wretched mortals," "dream figures." The birds conclude their appropriation of the anti-humanist rhetoric of archaic poetry by instructing the audience to pay attention—literally "apply the mind" [τὸν νοῦν]—to the true account of the nature and generation of the universe they are about to give (685–88). They tell of the origins of the gods and of cosmic phenomena in language that draws on Hesiod's *Theogony* and the cosmological poetry of Empedocles, and they follow this with a reminder that their migrations teach human beings the appropriate occasions for the various activities of agriculture and commerce. Their habits encode a kind of natural wisdom that is the

28. See the discussion of Crates's *Wild Animals*, above.

opposite of the sophists' inquisitive peering after what they cannot and ought not know, and for all these reasons, they are, they assert, "Ammon, Delphi, Dodona, and Phoebus Apollo" to human beings.

A chorus of birds reminds an audience of Athenian citizens of the heartbreaking nullity of human life as the poets who have come before them have imagined it, the futility of its efforts to rival the gods in their deathlessness, knowledge, and power. The audience, face to face with these marvelous beings, become the "sickly death's-heads" whom Odysseus addresses across the pit of blood that separates him from the ghosts in Hades. And yet, are their words their own, or are they merely parroting what Peisetairus has told them about their being older than the Titans and the Olympians?[29] Can we speak here of some kind of recovered knowledge, a quasi-Platonic recollection of what they had once known in times long ago, the memory of which has been reactivated by Peisetairus's prodding and which allows them to now claim that they "meditate imperishable things" (689)? And what of the agelessness and deathlessness they claim for themselves? Presumably they cannot understand it to refer to them as individuals, since they remain, after all, birds, subject to old age and death? Have they begun to think of themselves as a corporate body, a superorganism, as Peisetairus urged?

As Peisetairus sees it, the key to the birds' recovery of their former dominion, fictive or otherwise, is their possession of wings, which he views as a technology that they possess and he does not. He does not consider the birds' wings as a manifestation of their particular natures, a physiological development that allows them to pursue a life that is peculiarly their own, but as a tool with generalizable functions that he can appropriate for his own use. While Peisetairus may look ridiculous after Tereus's magical root allows him to sprout wings of his own (802–8), the absurdity is continuous with his own view of them as no more than a transferable prosthesis.

Peisetairus shows his hand in his initial fear of the birds. He alludes to the fable of the fox and the eagle in such a way that it is clear he sees their wings as a possession that makes them superior to him as things presently stand. The birds do not take the hint, however, and Tereus's root gives Peisetairus the specific difference he wishes to acquire (648–55). From this point on, he no

---

29. As Dunbar (1998, 291) argues. Aldo Leopold's "Marshland Elegy," which invites readers to hear the millennia of geological time in the voice of the crane, a survivor of the Eocene era, is also structured as a succession myth: once revered as the preferred sport of kings and emperors, cranes now "stand humbled, adrift in history," despised by their "new overlords," the small-minded farmers and developers who wreck their habitat and mock their peculiar appearance (see Leopold 1949, 95–101).

longer shows any fear of the birds, and begins to reveal his disdain for them as instruments of his own plan. Tereus's wife, the nightingale, who remained concealed when her husband sang her a tender erotic song earlier in the play, is brought on stage to be pawed and ogled. And when other human beings get wings, they will not use them to be birdlike, but to pursue their own affairs more efficiently. They will fly home to escape boring tragedies, to use the bathroom, or to commit adultery. As Peisetairus says, there's nothing funnier than being a bird (785–805).

The birds' subordination to Peisetairus is evident in the intruder scenes in which a number of human interlopers try to get him to pay for services to his new city. This sequence of lyric poet, oracle monger, geometer, city inspector, and decree seller (903–1057) is doubled by a series of applicants for birdship in the form of a father beater, a dithyrambic poet, and an informer (1337–1469), and in both cases it is Peisetairus alone who decides for the *polis*. Likewise, to the heroes and gods who solicit his favor—Iris (1196–1261), Prometheus (1494–1552) and the embassy that consists of Heracles, Poseidon, and the inarticulate divinity of the barbarian Triballians (1563–1693)—he is an absolute ruler: only his desires are addressed in the negotiations, not those of his subjects in whose interests the city was nominally founded.

The chorus of birds intervenes in these transactions with brief songs, but the reminders they contain of their distinctive forms of life as birds of the field and orchard (1058–71), and as birds of the meadow with particular seasonal behaviors (1088–1101), are marginal to the main stage business by which Peisetairus realizes his plan. As the gods are reduced to submission, so the birds are denatured by the inexorable logic of the comic plot. The reduction of their diversity to instrumental value is an occasion for hilarity in the long messenger speech that reports on the building of the city walls, which might serve as a parody of Aristotle's conception of political life as the pursuit of a common goal through division of labor: thirty thousand Libyan cranes swallowed stones for the foundations, corncrakes shaped them with their beaks, ten thousand storks made bricks, curlews and other river birds served as water carriers, geese shoveled clay with their feet, herons carried hods, ducks laid the finished bricks, swallows applied plaster with their tails, and woodpeckers finished off the carpentry (1133–57).

Birds, as nest makers, are natural builders; they do not become funny simply by working on a construction project. What is absurd is the degree to which their bodies have been instrumentalized, and this absurdity suggests that division of labor in the *polis*, in which each member of the collective performs a single, routinized task, is a top-down imposition on the life of a flocking or herding group in which each member pursues each of the activities appropriate to its kind. The scale of wonder tips away from the diversity of the birds toward the human intelligence that is able to make use of it, but, in doing so, it points to the social organization of other animals as a more satisfying form of collective life than the political existence on which human beings pride themselves.

The birds are complicit in their own diminishment. In their final songs, they catalogue the marvels of human life they have seen in their travels (1470–93, 1553–64, 1694–1705) and accede to their displacement as worthy objects of human attention. The real wonder is human society, and the birds become merely observers of its eccentricities. From this perspective, Peisetairus's roasting and eating, at the end of the play (1583, 1688), of individual birds who have rebelled against his new state is no more than a footnote to the progressive erasure of the birds as a whole in the unfolding of the comic plot. Even Tereus, the half-human, half-bird broker of Peisetairus's plan, is nowhere to be seen, for he vanishes from the stage when Peisetairus threatens to strip and abuse his wife. Tereus's last words—"let's go inside" (675)—are difficult to interpret, and might be staged in many ways, but he does not come back out after speaking them, and Peisetairus negotiates with the chorus leader instead.

Tereus disappears as Peisetairus assumes control and begins to produce a society that is geared toward the satisfaction of his own desires. His apotheosis as winged ruler of the universe (1731–65) is the opposite of the transformed state in which Tereus lived exhibiting characteristics of both human being and bird. Peisetairus simply takes what the birds have to offer him without participating in their nature, just as the human beings who would force their way into his new city are interested only in freedom from the laws of their own city, not in actually becoming birds. When Peisetarus informs a young man who has his heart set on the νόμοι (both laws and musical modes) of Cloudcuckooland that there is a great diversity of νόμοι among the birds, the young man turns out to be interested only in the antinomian opportunity to beat his father, not in extending his repertory of songs.

Euelpides too is nowhere to be seen in Peisetairus's kingdom. The "regressive and infantile fantasy" on which his heart was set is trumped by the "progressive and assertive fantasy of his companion."[30] There is, as it turns out, no going back. For Euelpides, whose idea was to find a city that would wrap

30. Perkell 1993, 3.

him like a warm, maternal blanket (122), the acquisition of wings turns out to be an evolutionary dead end, a maladaptation, even, that leaves him unable to compete with his companion in the new environment in which they find themselves. Peisetairus stands by himself in the series of intruder scenes that, in their unusual elaboration, point to the ethological kinship of this type of scene with nonhuman territorial defense.[31]

It has been argued that Peisetairus's success reaffirms the values of civic society in the face of romantic escapism.[32] And perhaps the end of the play does parade the usual forms of domination and subordination that exist in human societies at the expense of the distinctive ways of being in the world by which the birds had realized their own nature in action. But can we really call this an affirmation? To do so would be to ascribe unfulfilled ambition to animal life as a whole, for the birds of *Birds* are not merely ciphers for human behavior, as the wasps of *Wasps* stand for the unrelenting quarrelsomeness of old men addicted to the law courts. They are present as birds in the earlier parts of the play, with their own forms of social organization, and this vision of zoological sociality continues to encompass and interrogate the human society that takes center stage at the end.

Individual appetite held in check by power is not a model that describes all forms of animal sociality, and the triumph of one two-footed wonder over another that occurs in the play should not be reproduced as a paean to dominion on the part of its maker. Incest, in the Tereus myth, is what tells us the hero has lost his grip on the abstentions that define what it is to be human. Cannibalism is the punishment meted out for this crime and what puts the criminal beyond the pale of all forms of social life.[33] And it is as a cannibal that Peisetairus stands before us at the end of play. As he eats the flesh of his polity, he has become the overseer of his own evils, the post–human being in whose quest he set out at the beginning of the play. He is, as Aeschylus reminds us, an unholy thing: "For how can a bird be sanctified if it eats another bird?"[34]

---

31. Cf. Ardrey: "A territory is an area of space, whether of water or earth or air, which an animal or group of animals defends as an exclusive preserve . . . In most but not all territorial species, defense is directed only against fellow members of the kind. A squirrel does not regard as mouse as a trespasser" (1966, 3). It is the unusual fact that Peisetairus has to defend his space against gods as well as men that is, in *Birds*, so revealing of the typical situation.

32. Ceccarelli 2000, 463.

33. Forbes Irving 1990, 103.

34. ὄρνιθος ὄρνις πῶς ἂν ἁγνεύοι φαγών (Aeschylus *Suppliants* 226).

ISHMAEL'S WHALES

As Athenian comedy developed, it shed its fantastic elements. The disaffected citizen who turned his back on human society no longer encountered wild men or animals outside it, who presented him with alternatives to the familiar norms of human sociality; instead, he met with well-intentioned efforts on the part of his family and friends to soothe his savage soul. He became a misanthrope, a problem character, not a voyager to unknown realms.[35] What is lost in this transition is what commentators often lose sight of at the end of *Birds*. As the focus narrows to human beings alone, their society is no longer seen against the larger horizon of zoological sociality. The alienated man becomes a melancholic in need of repair and reintegration, and nature a desert, consoling to him insofar as human beings are absent from it, but a place to find solitude, not the company of other animals.

The loss of possibilities for human self-understanding that comes with the elimination of Old Comedy's talking animals can be gauged from two modern stories in which a human being's encounter with animal sociality changes his understanding of the zoological basis of human society. Herman Melville's *Moby-Dick* begins, like *Birds*, with one unhappy citizen. Ishmael has so much pent-up aggression toward his fellow Manhattanites that murder and suicide dominate his thoughts. His desire to go to sea is a substitute for the "pistol and ball" he would otherwise aim at them or himself (1:93).[36] He sees his irritation as a physiological condition induced by too close a proximity to other members of his own species, its cure a reenchantment with the world to be effected by an encounter with its most impressive nonhuman inhabitants, and the mysterious individual who is preeminent among them:

> The great flood-gates of the wonder-world swung open, and in the wild conceits that swayed me to my purpose, two and two there floated into my inmost soul, endless processions of the whale, and, mid most of them all, one grand hooded phantom, like a snow hill in the air. (1:98)

Ishmael imagines whales as social animals from the outset, and his vision of Moby-Dick as an individual hemmed in by his fellow creatures mirrors his understanding of his own place among men. His desire to meet the whale

35. Menander's *Dyskolos* is the best-preserved example of the type; on the development, see Ceccarelli (2000, 463).
36. Melville 1972 (see chapter 2, note 1).

is not fueled by hatred of him, as Ahab's is, but by a desire to see his own suppressed aggression toward other men writ large in its gigantic counterpart in the society of animals.[37] By the time he gets to sea, however, Ishmael's aggression has been dissipated by his friendship with Queequeg, the "soothing savage" (10:146), and Ahab becomes the instantiation of social isolation, his solitary confinement in his cabin reflecting a psychic autonomy figured as a machine that runs without the need for human intervention (36:259).[38]

Ishmael's free and easy intimacy with Queequeg contrasts with Ahab's analysis of his own relationship with his crew, in which he casts himself as the "cogged circle" that "fits into all their various wheels" and makes them revolve to his bidding (37:266). Without fixed ideas, and susceptible to outside impressions, Ishmael is well suited to become one of the few who can give "a truthful idea of the living whale as seen by his living hunters" (56:372), and so offer a corrective to contemporary cetology, which is imaginatively unpersuasive because it is inattentive to zoological reality.[39] Ishmael's understanding advances with his opportunities for close observation. At first, when the *Pequod* comes upon a large party of right whales, he can barely perceive them as animate beings. He sees "vast black forms" that look "more like lifeless masses of rock than anything else" and compares himself with elephant hunters who mistake their prey for "blackened elevations of the soil." Creatures of such size, he concludes, rule out the sympathetic feelings one might have for a dog or a horse, particularly when they live in the sea, and their affects are remote and inaccessible. "Where," he asks, "does the ocean furnish any fish that in disposition answers to the sagacious kindness of the dog?" (58:379).

37. For Ahab-centered readings that see the pursuit of Moby-Dick as a manifestation of mid-century American appetite for destruction, see Marx (1964, 295–96); Buell (2001, 222); and especially Slotkin (1973, 538–50). Cf. Zoellner (1973, 146–90), who contrasts Ahab's hatred with the process by which Ishmael comes to observe, understand and sympathize with the whales he encounters. For a recent defense of Ahab's use of Moby-Dick as a symbolic object that enables a range of human social practices, see Evans (2003, 138–50), who includes a defense of her defense in light of the catastrophic outcome of Ahab's pursuit.

38. Ausband (1975, 211). Psychic autonomy all too easily turns into psychic automatism, and the likely outcome of Ahab's is prefigured in "The Town-Ho's Story," in which Radney's obsessive hatred of Steelkilt becomes a predestined death at his hands (54.352).

39. D. G. Burnett (2007, 101–6) discusses Ishmael's "wry and dismissive commentary on learned cetology" (103) in the context of professional whalemen's contributions to contemporary scientific debates as to whether whales were fish; as he notes, their ideas about their prey were not always the outcome of unmediated encounters with the animals themselves, for some at least were as discriminating readers of zoology as Vincent (1949) showed Melville to have been.

It is by witnessing the deaths of whales that Ishmael comes to understand that they are "instinct in all parts with the same sort of life that lives in a dog or a horse." As boats from the *Pequod* and the rival *Jungfrau* overtake a straggler from a pod of sperm whales, he sees that this outsider is a sick old male, covered with strange encrustations, lacking one of his fins, and flatulent. As he struggles to elude his pursuers, he looks like a bird with a clipped wing, "making affrighted broken circles in the air, vainly striving to escape the piratical hawks," but unlike the bird, which has a voice, "and with plaintive cries will make known her fear," this "vast brute of the sea" is silent, his fear "chained up and enchanted in him" (81:459–62).

The whale lacks the power to express his terror as sound, but it is apparent in his choking respiration, an "unspeakably pitiable" sight that is "enough to appal the stoutest man who so pitied" (81:459–62). Ishmael's cathexis to the greatest beasts of the sea does not occur in response to the undaunted aggression of the greatest among them, as he had imagined, but in witnessing the effects of social exclusion and incapacity upon one of the least. Once this connection is made, his imagination works freely, as he endeavors to think his way into the hunted animal's perceptual experience: "Who can tell how appalling to the wounded whale must have been such huge phantoms flitting over his head!" The success of his efforts is rendered by the sympathetic movement of Melville's prose as it registers Ishmael's feelings for the whale as he dies from the injuries he has sustained:

> So spent was he by loss of blood, that he helplessly rolled away from the wreck he had made; lay panting on his side, impotently flapped with his stumped fin, then over and over slowly revolved like a waning world; turned up the white secrets of his belly; lay like a log, and died. (81: 464–66)

Sympathetic experience of the whale's death impels Ishmael to studious appreciation of its physiological differences from himself in the chapter devoted to its tail that follows soon after. This detailed naturalistic description differs from his earlier account of a whale's eye and ear (74:438) in that it is not so much an expression of sheer wonder as it is an effort to think his way into the animal's everyday existence by imagining how it uses a nonhuman body to pursue a life of emotions and goal-oriented behaviors he now knows are continuous with his own (86:484).[40]

40. Cf. Zoellner 1973, 163–65.

Ishmael concludes "The Tail" by asserting that some aspects of whales' lives must remain closed to him because whales do not have faces in which expressions can be observed (86:487). In "The Grand Armada," however, he is able to look at the social and familial life of a large group of sperm whales from very close up, and as he does so, he is able to discern affects that were inaccessible to him from the head of a single dead animal. Ishmael does not regard what he sees as an immutable form of instinctual behavior. Rather, the gathering of these whales in large companies is, as he understands it, a historically specific adaptation of their social organization that the whales have adopted in response to human predation, which has recently assumed unprecedented levels:[41]

> But here be it premised, that owing to the unwearied activity with which of late they have been hunted over all four oceans, the Sperm Whales, instead of almost invariably sailing in small detached companies, as in former times, are now frequently met with in extensive herds, some-times embracing so great a multitude, that it would almost seem as if numerous nations of them had sworn solemn league and covenant for mutual assistance and protection. (87:490)

As in Aristotle's description of bird communication, the emphasis here falls upon perception: the way the whales behave as a group leads Ishmael to posit a certain level of understanding among them. Although this is a hypothesis that cannot be tested, it is important because of the further exercise of the imagination it enables. The initial observation generates increasingly ambitious analogies between the sociality of the whales and human society: their "host of vapory spouts" shows like "the cheerful chimneys of some dense metropolis"; their "vast fleet" hurries on "as marching armies, approaching an unfriendly defile in the mountains, accelerate their march"; when attacked, they panic like human beings who "when herded together in the sheepfold of a theater's pit," will "at the slightest alarm of fire, rush helter-skelter for the outlets"; their cows and calves look as if they had been "purposely locked up" in their innermost ranks, as in a human nursery; when amorous and "over-

41. This point is missed by Armstrong (2004, 1053), who accuses Melville of unconsciously naturalizing the gender ideology of mid-nineteenth-century America. Sperm whales, in fact, are famous for the doting behavior of female caregivers, including mothers, aunts, and grand-mothers, in what are properly called nurseries (forms of enclosure that shield infant whales from external predation). Investigation of the historically specific forms of nurturing display within these nurseries is an emerging field of cetological research (see Siebert 2009).

flowing with mutual esteem," they salute one another *"more hominum,"* amid "submarine bridal-chambers"; when wounded, one moves among his fellows "like the lone mounted desperado Arnold at the battle of Saratoga, carrying dismay wherever he went" (87:490–99).

From "Cutting In" to "The Sphynx," Melville shows us the operations of a human group configured as a kind of lethal superorganism whose single-minded intention is to separate the constituents of another animal's body into what is profitable to itself and what it can discard without loss. In "The Grand Armada," by contrast, we witness an individual human imagination moving outward from sympathetic understanding of how another animal's body works to a catalogue-like fantasia on the kinds of life this body enables. The sexual fecundity Ishmael observes in the whale nursery generates exuberant mental fecundity of his own, as birth and parenting inspire his most rapturous interrogations of what human beings and whales share:

> As human infants while suckling will calmly and fixedly gaze away from the breast, as if leading two different lives at the same time; and while yet drawing mortal nourishment, be still spiritually feasting upon some unearthly reminiscence; even so did the young of these whales seem looking up towards us, but not at us, as if we were but a bit of Gulf-weed in their new-born sight. (87:497)

In his account of the hunted whale, Ishmael gives us the animal's view of the dark, unintelligible shapes passing above its head. Here, the whale's eye view is no view, the impossibility of grasping the mental representations that appear in an infant's feeding or the recollection of pre-incarnate experience. Such thoughts are lost to the adult mind; while the infants gaze upward and outward, their parents are "quietly eyeing" the sailors who look at their offspring with no more understanding of their pleasures than they themselves have.

CÉLINE'S CHILDREN, CÉLINE'S BIRDS

Ishmael's encounter with whale sociality allows his understanding of other forms of life to go beyond the fantasies of destructive aggression that motivate his departure from Manhattan. As I noted in the previous chapter, Melville himself was conscious of the fact that the relentless pursuit of other animals was becoming less and less of a heroic endeavor in his own time. In the first chapter of *The Confidence-Man*, he anticipates the killing of America's last wolves, and, in *Moby-Dick*, he entertains the idea that sperm whales may be wiped out by human beings, only to conclude, ironically enough, that they will likely escape total annihilation by shifting their habitat to the polar ice caps, "two firm fortresses, which, in all human probability, will for ever remain impregnable" (105:573).[42]

Melville leaves open the possibility that even his worst estimates of human destructiveness might fall short of future realities, and his prescience is confirmed in the identification of unrestrained destructiveness with humanness itself in the novels of Louis-Ferdinand Céline. His last, *Rigadoon*, is dedicated "To the Animals," and, in recounting the flight of its author, his partner Lili, and their cat Bébert, from the Allied bombing of northern Germany at the end of the Second World War, it shows a quite distinctive form of attention to the modes of sociality present in nonhuman animals and the kinds of communication by which they are enabled. So, as the flat cars on which Céline and his companions are riding come to a halt somewhere outside Hamburg, they see on the train tracks a group of mentally handicapped children who have emerged from the tarps in which they were wrapped and are now wandering in search of food. Céline and Lili have nothing to offer them, so they show them their cat instead:

> she takes him out of his bag . . . ah, now they're interested . . . they laugh . . . I mean they screw up their noses and drool even more . . . they want to play with Bébert! . . . no! . . . mustn't! . . . but Bébert wants to play with them . . . so bad that he miows . . . and the kids cry . . . let's get this over with.[43]

The children do not look entirely human, and Céline adopts the abbreviated speech adults use to animals and infants, less in the hope that it will be effective than in recognition of the fact that other kinds are not. Bébert and the children, however, have no problems communicating with one another,

---

42. Cf. Schultz (2000, 98–99, 106–9). It is worth comparing Melville's vision of the polar ice caps as a place that might yet shelter forms of life capable of destroying human beings *en masse* with H. P. Lovecraft's "At the Mountains of Madness." Lovecraft's story, in which a polar expedition awakens a society of nonhuman beings from age-long dormancy, is written as a scientific report whose concluding recommendation is that "some of earth's dark, dead corners and unplumbed depths be let alone, lest sleeping abnormalities wake to resurgent life" (Lovecraft 2005, 585). The story is a kind of nightmare version of *Walden*: in wildness is not the preservation of humanity, but its well-deserved destruction. Lovecraft's antihumanism is analyzed admiringly by Houellebecq (2005, 57–62, 115–19).

43. Céline 1997, 171.

and Céline identifies the unwillingness of adult human beings to heed forms of communication other than their own as the origin of the unending violence of dominion, one manifestation of which is the war itself:

> To tell you the truth, these kids, so feebleminded, so dribbling and drooling, couldn't ask for anything . . . we could only see they were trying to tell us something . . . there wouldn't be any more slaughterhouses if the officials in charge took a look at the eyes of the feebleminded . . . naturally wars go on and on . . . the same brutes keep it up on both sides. (171–72)

Céline claimed his novels were not fictions, but rather an effort to capture in the carefully worked measures of his prose, "the only reality that counts," the "secret, discreet, biological reality you can't see and can't hear" (192). Like the metrical experiments of Hipponax and Williams Carlos Williams, his prose rhythms are an attempt to communicate anthropological truth as somatic event.[44] From this perspective, his encounter with the children records a double alienation. Both Céline and the children are exiles from the normal forms of human society, but the children are a distinctive zoological community of their own, and they exhibit a relaxed sociality with one another and with Bébert in which he cannot participate. In addition, their "slobber," "bubbles," and "bark" are the direct expression of somatic experience to which Céline aspired in his own prose, but which can only be represented indirectly in discourse subject to syntax and semantics.

Céline and the children eventually part company, and he, Lili, and Bébert go on to Copenhagen. They visit a city park, which begins to take on a strange and unfamiliar aspect as they wander in it, as if it were a wilderness at the edge of human habitation, not a green space in the midst of it. They lose their way in the woods and sit down in a deserted spot from which they can see the ruins of a demolished castle, but not a single person. It is the end of their journey, and from a secret compartment in their traveling bag they take the tokens of their identity that have been hidden during their flight: two passports, a marriage certificate, and a lady's pistol. We are ready for the end of the novel, but at this point something surprising happens:

---

44. Cf. Céline: "I am not a man of ideas. I am a man of style" (1999, 10). Kristeva discusses this style as an effort to "raise neural and biological experience up to social contract and communication" (1982, 188–206).

over there in the grass, a bird . . . but not the usual kind of bird . . . "collector's item," I'd say, from the Jardin des Plantes . . . about the size of a duck, half pink, half black . . . and ruffled! feathers every which way . . . I look further . . . another! that one I know! . . . I saw him first! . . . an ibis . . . fancy meeting you here! . . . and an egret! . . . certainly not from Denmark! and now a peacock . . . they've come here on purpose! . . . and a lyre bird . . . they want something to eat . . . it's not a very nourishing spot, ruins, brambles, and stones . . . still another! . . . a toucan! . . . they're only ten fifteen feet away . . . they'd make friends if we had something to give them, but we really haven't got a thing . . . (256)

That *Rigadoon* ends where Aristophanes' *Birds* begins is obvious enough, but what to make of this apparently fantastic encounter in the work of an author who disclaimed invention?[45] A naturalistic answer is at hand: the birds "must have come from down south like us, from zoos in Germany, bombed." Like Céline, Lili, and Bébert, and like the "little cretins," the birds are a band of fugitives. They are a strange assortment from every corner of the globe, and, like Ishmael's whales, they are doing their best to maintain a form of sociality in the face of multiple experiences of human aggression—first the zoo, and now the war. Céline and Lili "haven't got a thing" to offer the birds, who instead seem to offer them a kind of hope. For they get to their feet, confident all of a sudden that they can make their way out of the park, back "where we came from . . . we'll find the way . . ." (256).

Céline's wonder at the social groups of other animals stops short of an attempt to join them, and lingers instead in the moment when this possibility is most tantalizing—undiminished, that is to say, by what we might learn from them if we were able to understand their communication. Peisetairus discovers that birds, so diverse in their forms, are in fact subject to the same motivations as human beings. Céline, by contrast, keeps alive the fantasies that are enabled by the absence of a common language. There is no descent into banality, and Bébert, the children, and the birds remain on the other side of a threshold the author cannot cross without ceasing to be human.

45. Although he admired Aristophanes' inventiveness; see Céline (2006, 35).

CHAPTER FOUR

Changing Bodies

Being and Becoming an Animal in Semonides, Ovid,
and H. P. Lovecraft

Only the mind of a philosopher grows wings—and rightly so.
—Plato, *Phaedrus*

Athenian Old Comedy does not balk at the hurdles of sympathetic imagination with which human beings hedge their curiosity about the lives of other
animals. Its response to the desire to know is simply to invent: it offers strong
forms of fictionality as a satisfaction of natural wonder. This is the source
both of its instant dramatic impact and the imaginative discontents that follow
in its wake. The language barrier separating human beings from other animals
is removed, and Peisetarus and Euelpides are able to join the society of birds,
but what they discover as a result is that the animals whose society they have
joined are just like human beings. Ishmael too discovers that whales are not
the fantastic beasts of his hunting imagination but live in social groups much
like those he has left behind. Only Céline does not foreclose fantasies of difference with the discovery of sameness in the social group.

In this chapter, I want to explore a set of poems in which the difference
missed in the social group is found to be present in the individual body. It
includes narratives of metamorphosis, in which a human body is transformed into that of another animal by some form of external agency, as well
as some less familiar poems in which an animal inhabits a human body, and
what is most characteristically human is found in the body of an animal.
These poems enact the possibility that human beings' experiences of the
life forms they encounter in their everyday interactions—their own bodies
included—are in some sense flawed, partial, or necessarily incomplete, and

so subject to punitive correction. I conclude with a discussion of the relationship between misrecognition and the desire for otherness in narratives of evolutionary theory.

THE PROPER STUDY OF MANKIND

Poetry claiming to discern human persons in animal bodies and animal persons in human bodies requires omniscient intervention into human and nonhuman interiority. The claim that poetry's narrativization of divinity is an illegitimate intrusion into a form of life it can only misrepresent is coeval with literary criticism itself: Plato's indignation at Homer's representation of the gods is well known, and there is no need to rehearse his criticisms here. But animals raise different questions, and it is worth returning to Aristotle's account of poetic narrative as representative human behavior in the *Poetics* to see how it handles kinds of ontological difference.

As Stephen Halliwell observes, Aristotle makes a transition from a general account of mimesis in the first chapter of the *Poetics* to a discussion of the proper subject matter of poetry in the second "with a brevity which should provoke careful scrutiny."[1] One question we might ask is how the acknowledgment of the role of poetic mimesis in the representation of nonhuman life in the first chapter, witnessed by the reference to Chaeremon's polymetric drama *The Centaur*, becomes, in the opening of the second, the assertion that "since mimetic artists represent people in action, it is necessary that these people be either elevated or base"—particularly since Aristotle refers immediately afterward to post-classical representations of Cyclopses in the work of the dithyrambic poets Timotheus and Philoxenus. The argument that poetry is, or ought to be, fiction does not entail that its subjects must be human beings, but, since it is assumed that they are, we must investigate the conflation of these desiderata.

Aristotle asserts that there are three ways in which poetry as a verbal medium can represent the behavior of human beings:

καὶ γὰρ ἐν τοῖς αὐτοῖς καὶ τὰ αὐτὰ μιμεῖσθαι ἔστιν ὁτὲ μὲν ἀπαγγέλουντα ἢ ἕτερόν τι γιγνόμενον ὥσπερ Ὅμηρος ποιεῖ, ἢ ὡς τὸν αὐτὸν καὶ μὴ μεταβάλλοντα, ἢ πάντας ὡς πράττοντας καὶ ἐνεργοῦντας τοὺς μιμουμένους. (*Poetics* 2, 1448a19)

---

1. Halliwell 1987, 73.

[In representing the same things in the same medium it is possible to do so by reporting them at one moment and becoming something different at another, as Homer does, or by remaining oneself without undergoing a change, or by staging all the agents of the narrative as actors and performers.]

Aristotle adapts terminology proposed by Socrates in Book 3 of the *Republic*, where he claims that a story may be told as pure narration, in which only the poet speaks, mixed, in which the presentation alternates, as it does in Homer, between the poet's voice and the voices of his characters, and drama, in which only the characters speak and the poet's voice is not heard. Unlike Socrates, however, Aristotle states a preference for poets and poetic forms in which character speech is maximized: Homer is the best of epic poets because he cedes the stage to his characters and lets them do the talking, and drama is better still, because this is all it consists of (*Poetics* 24). Maximization of character speech avoids the declarative temptations of first person poetic forms and lets audiences enjoy their emotional engagement with the characters without undue interruption. Since gods are conventionally believed to be capable of using human speech to communicate with human beings, their occasional appearances in epic and drama do not distract the audience, so long as their actions are not unduly fantastic, in which case a place can always be found for them as an excess of poetic imagination.[2]

Aristotle's assertion that the agents of poetic narrative will be types of human beings looks like a reasonable consequence of his account of the value of poetic mimesis. All the same, Platonic fears about the dangers of imitation linger on in the *Poetics*. Aristotle speaks of the poet who creates fictional speakers "becoming something different" when he does so, and of the poet who refrains from such dramatization "remaining himself without undergoing a change." Fully imagined staging of another being is a form of metamorphosis, and we hear in the background of this claim Socrates' belief that participatory involvement in literary representations "feeds up and makes strong" nonhuman affects that ought to be denied the nourishment they need to survive (*Republic* 10, 606a–d). For as the myth of Er reminds us, the life of Ajax is really that of a lion, Agamemnon's that of an eagle, Thersites' that of a monkey.

2. Cf. Payne 2007, 7–9.

ANIMALS IN HUMAN PLACES

Poetry, as Socrates sees it, hybridizes human beings by fostering alien life forms within them and putting the lives of other animals where the human ought to be. Socrates' account of what poetry does to human beings is continuous with what poetry knows about them in the work of ancient poets themselves. I begin with fragment 7 of Semonides, because its revelations begin in the home: its premise is that marriage is not a union between two human beings, but between a husband who is fully human and a wife who, despite her human appearance, is in fact something nonhuman in human form. Rather than emerging from stray encounters in the wilderness, negotiation of the relationship between the human and the nonhuman is renewed every day in the bedroom, the kitchen, and the living room. Ontological errors and epistemological doubt are with human beings at the dinner table and when they make love, and what the poem suggests is that these uncertainties not only secure the erotic attachment between human couples, but hold together the collectives of which they are a part.

The poem is preserved in the anthology of the Byzantine Stobaeus in a section entitled "On Marriage: Abuse of Women" (Stobaeus 4.22), and modern scholars have generally agreed with him in treating it as a misogynistic tirade while—unlike him—deploring the excesses of its satirical fulminations.[3] The opening lines, however, make it difficult to locate the poem in the tradition of iambic aggression exemplified by Archilochus and Hipponax. For they begin with the assertion that "in the beginning the god made the mind of woman separately [χωρίς]"—either separately from the mind of men, or in distinct kinds among women themselves.[4] This is not a personal narrative: there is no indication that its author has been wounded by his subjects and has hostile intentions toward them as a result. He is not abject, and he does not speak with the warmth of loathing, but links his poem to cooler didactic traditions of mythical exposition, and advice for living in the world that comes from knowing how things really stand there—the poems of Hesiod are the best-known examples.

After this solemn start, the poet claims that the god made one woman "from a slender-whiskered pig," and that this woman, smothered in mud, lies around all over the place in her house, rolling on the floor in her dirty

---

3. This distaste is usually combined with the detection of formal shortcomings so that the author can be portrayed as an all round failure; see Verdenius (1968, 138); Schear (1984, 39).

4. See Loraux (1993, 90–91). I cite the poem from the edition of West (1971).

clothes and sitting on the dung heap getting fat (1–6). He made another out of a wicked vixen, and this one is inquisitive about everything. However, while "nothing good or bad escapes her attention," she changes her mind constantly as to which is which, since her mood is different at different times (7–11). A third woman is made from a dog, and this one wants to hear and see everything; she wanders around everywhere, barking and intruding where she is not wanted. A husband cannot put a stop to her noise with threats, whether he gets angry and knocks out her teeth with a stone, or whether he speaks to her gently. Even if she is sitting with their friends she keeps up a whine he can do nothing about (12–20).

The first of these animals seems readily metaphorical. As a way of suggesting that immersion in sensual enjoyment is best understood through its nonhuman exemplars, the pig derives its special authority from the pleasure it takes in substances human beings find repulsive, so that its pleasure interrogates the human delights with which it is analogous. The success of Marie Darrieussecq's *Pig Tales*—the life of a pig woman told by the human animal herself—points to the continuing fascination this form of animal life exerts:

> There's nothing better than warm earth around you when you wake up
> in the morning, the smell of your own body mingling with the odor of
> the humus, the first mouthfuls you take without even getting up, gob-
> bling acorns, chestnuts, everything that has rolled down into the wallow
> while you were scrabbling in your dreams.[5]

Exaggeration reveals the conflict of desire and repulsion toward a behavior that is strictly regimented by human social codes: the answer to Johnny Burke's question, in "Swinging on a Star"—"Would you rather be a pig?"—might turn out to be yes.[6] It may not seem obvious to consider inquisitiveness and compulsiveness as forms of desire, but the poem's version of the lives of fox and dog imagines them as such. The fox woman's life is one of unlimited inquiry and comment, freed from the need to base one's comments on consistent judgment. This understanding of her behavior matches Pindar's claim that Archilochus's foxiness is merely ceaseless carping that cannot disclose anything true because it originates in mood or temper. Conversely, the

5. Darrieussecq 1997, 150–51.

6. In the terms of Deleuze and Guattari, the pig "deterritorializes" a human appetite by remapping it onto the habitat and behavior of another animal. While the intention may be construed as satirical, such representations fantasize a "line of escape" from social constraints because they envisage the maximal pursuit of the desire in question (1986, 35).

dog woman's life is a hyperbolic version of care, vigilance over the household imagined as an anxious obsession that enrages the husband she means to serve.

At this point Semonides changes tack and moves from the animal world to the elements.[7] The Olympians made a woman from earth and gave her to men disabled or impaired (πηρόν; compare with πηλός = mud). This woman is completely indifferent to value terms; she knows nothing of good and evil, and of the activities of human beings she knows only how to eat. Her indifference to herself and her surroundings is such that even in the cold of winter she does not pull her chair up to the fire (21–26).[8] In contrast to the pig woman, whose eating is a manifestation of uncontrolled sensuality, this woman's consumption is a mechanical process that lacks interiority of any kind, just as the larger issues of human life provoke no cognitive activity in her. Unlike the hyperactive curiosity of the fox and dog women, the earth woman is sheer matter without inner functioning: no one is piloting the machine.[9]

In addition to the earth woman, there is an ocean woman, who is always in two minds. One day she smiles and is cheerful, so that any guest who sees her in her husband's house will praise her for being beautiful and good. On another day, however, she is unendurable even to look upon and rages "like a bitch around her children," implacable and evil-tempered to friends and foes alike. So, we are told, the sea is often mild and harmless—"a great delight to sailors in the summer time"—but often rages too, "rolling around with loudly beating waves" (27–40).

If the earth woman imagines a form of human life without human cognitive and emotional activity, the sea woman imagines one in which they seem to be present, but in fact are only behaviors, not manifestations of the thinking and feeling subject to which they ought to testify. When the sea woman storms and smiles, her actions cannot be understood as expressions of anger and delight. She may act like a dog defending its young on any given day, but this behavior is not a response to threat any more than variations in the surface of

---

7. Hubbard (1994) suggests that the earth and water women reflect an awareness of Ionian elemental theory on the part of the poet. His discussion of the poem's transformation formulas should be compared with that of Loraux (1993, 96–97), who sees their origin in the genetic theory of Hesiod.

8. I accept Schneidewin's proposal for the beginning of line 25: κοὐδ' ἦν κακὸν χειμῶνα ποιήσῃ θεός.

9. The earth woman is reminiscent of the Mayan myth in which the gods, in an early effort at creation, fashion out of mud a race of human beings who are too inert to praise them; see Tedlock (1985, 69–86).

the sea reveal the changing thoughts and emotions of a mind from which they issue. The sea woman has a nature (φυήν) that is changeable, not a temper (ὀργήν) like the fox.[10]

Semonides' excursus among the elements points to continuities of appetitive and affective behavior between human beings and other animals by imagining forms of life that do not share them. He returns to animals with a woman whom the gods made from "the ash-colored ass that is patient of blows." This woman does acceptable work around the house, but only when compelled to do so. She eats in an inner room by day, and at night she eats in front of the fire. She does not mind who she has sex with, for she thinks of sex as work (ἔργον ἀφροδίσιον) and, since she is as resigned to erotic labor as she is to other kinds of housework, she accepts whoever comes along (43–50).

Contrast with the earth woman's indifference reveals the ass woman's resignation as a passion in disguise; hers is a "line of escape" into pure submission, animal existence imagined as willed endurance in physical labor and the nutritional activities that sustain it. Intertextually, her links are with Ajax, imagined as an ass consciously indifferent to the blows that rain down on it in his deliberate retreat from the Trojans (*Iliad* 11.558–62), and the tender virgin of Hesiod's *Works and Days*, who curls up in the warmth of an inner room during winter storms when the octopus gnaws its foot for food at the bottom of the sea (519–25). We see a body wrapped in protective enclosures, and the self inside it similarly secure from the forces that rage around outside. The implication of these textual memories points to the ass woman's conception of her own body as a place of refuge into which she can retreat and feel herself untouched in her inmost core by the powers that have dominion over her.

Next is a woman who comes from a weasel or cat (γαλῆ),[11] a wretched and pitiful creature, because there is nothing about her that is beautiful, desirable, delightful, or erotic. Like the ass woman, she will give herself to any man who happens to be around (τὸν ἄνδρα τὸν παρεόντα) but, unlike her, she is crazy for sex, an appetite she is unable to satisfy fully because she sickens whoever she is with. If the ass woman's behavior is resignation to other people's desires, the same behavior in the cat woman is the piratical pursuit of her own. Just as she commandeers passersby to satisfy her sexual needs, in spite of their repugnance, so she steals from her neighbors and gobbles down the remnants of half-consumed sacrifices (50–56). In contrast to the earth woman

---

10. This contrast disappears if the emendations proposed by Lloyd-Jones (1975, 72–73) and Pellizer and Tedeschi (1990, 129–30) are adopted.

11. See Lloyd-Jones (1975, 76–77) on the arguments for one or the other.

who is indifferent to value terms, the cat woman is their negation; denied the satisfactions that others find inside society, she seizes her pleasures on its margins instead.

The cat woman is followed by a woman whose attractions are universally acknowledged, the offspring of a "luxurious, long-haired mare." She avoids all housework and any possibility of getting her hands dirty, but her refusal to do chores in no way diminishes her desirability. While the ass woman has to be compelled to work (ἀνάγκη), the horse woman compels her husband to love her (ἀνάγκη) in spite of her refusal to work, though the compulsion here is not brute force but erotic charm: she is simply too attractive to refuse. She washes and perfumes herself two or three times a day, and her hair is always beautifully arranged and adorned with flowers. She is a lovely sight to others, though a thing of evil to whoever possesses her, unless that person is a king or tyrant who is able to enjoy such useless possessions (57–70).

The horse obviously figures beauty as an attribute of high status households in contrast to the humble domestic economy in which the ass performs its labors. Other landmarks of the ordinary working home also reappear in this section as domestic territories the horse woman shuns: the dung heap in which the pig woman revels and the hearth before which the ass woman loves to eat are both avoided by her for fear of dirtying herself. The freedom from work that is the result of the horse woman's good looks means she has no need to consciously formulate her desires or to pursue them in deliberate opposition to the life she ought to lead. She requires no line of escape because no one interferes with her preferred activities. Her freedom flows from her bloodlines: she is as her mother horse gave birth to her, and her behavior is not so much a refusal of labor as an unreflective expression of what she is by nature, a fascinating sight (θέημα), like the sea woman on her good days.[12]

Not so the monkey woman, the worst of all those that Zeus has given to men. Her face is hatefully ugly, and she is an object of ridicule to everyone who sees her as she walks through town. Her neck is short, she walks with difficulty, and her legs end without buttocks. Her ugliness, like the horse woman's beauty, is recognized by all, and her husband is pitied above all men because he is obliged to sleep with her. If the horse woman's ostentation is the unselfconscious behavior of a beautiful and valued animal whose desires are immediately gratified by its caregivers, the monkey woman's public appearances combine self-display with an awkward approximation of ordinary

---

12. The peasant farmer Strepsiades likewise thinks of his son's unreflective love of horses as a biological inheritance from his aristocratic mother in Aristophanes' *Clouds* (59–74).

human capacities in a way that evokes hostility from those who witness them. This hostility provokes aggression of her own: like a monkey, she knows all kinds of tricks, and she spends her time plotting "how she can do as much harm as possible" (71–82).

The destructive stratagems of the monkey woman are contrasted with the domestic arts of the wife with whom the catalogue ends, the bee woman. The husband of this woman alone is able to manage his household successfully, since she attends to its resources. She loves her husband and is loved by him in return, and she grows old as the mother of a lovely and famous family (83–87). But there are problems here too. Bees, for Aristotle, are among the animals that exhibit a development of political sociality analogous to human society's progression from the household to the city. However, the bee woman's value as a wife is measured by the defectiveness of her social interactions with other women; she "takes no pleasure in sitting among women where they tell erotic stories." If Zeus has favored certain men with such wives as "the best and most sensible women," it is at the price of a social group larger than the household being able to pursue a common goal through gendered division of labor.[13]

So the catalogue ends, and Semonides follows it with some general remarks on the obstacles a wife presents to the successful conduct of a man's everyday life. A wife consumes his wealth, her quick and fickle temper makes it hard for him to relax at home or invite friends over, and her deceitfulness turns him into a laughing stock. For while every man disparages the outrageous behavior of his neighbor's wife, he fails to see how he is tricked by his own. Despite the inconveniences wives entail, however, husbands have been bound to them with unbreakable chains "ever since Hades welcomed those who fought over a wife" (94–118)—a reference to the various contests for the hand of Helen that points to the venerable ancestry of the mix of irrational attachment and domestic torment with which the poem concerns itself.

The poem's final lines recapitulate the perspective from which sexual difference is viewed in it: how can men and women live together as husbands and wives, and how do other members of society view their cohabitation?[14]

---

13. In contrast to Allen (2000, 120), I would suggest that Semonides' bee woman indicates how difficult animals are to think with as tropes for normative values: some aspect of their lives always eludes its discursive reduction, and what is repressed has a way of returning to cancel the intended symbolism.

14. Cf. Schear (1984, 41), although the attempt to establish a precise performance context for the poem (a kind of archaic stag night) on the basis of this observation strikes me as misguided; cf. Brown (1997, 75) and my discussion of Osborne (2001) below.

By way of conclusion, I want to focus on the zoanthropic approach the poem takes to these issues: what is ultimately at stake in its claim that women's bodies live nonhuman lives?

Semonides' poem has affinities with the kind of folktale known as the animal bride story. In such tales, a female animal marries a human groom only to reveal herself on the wedding night or shortly thereafter as an animal and not a human being.[15] In an example from the Aesopic tradition, a cat falls in love with a handsome man and is made into a woman by Aphrodite. The man she desires reciprocates her love and they are married. However, at the wedding feast the cat woman spies a mouse, and leaps from her seat to chase it, ending the young man's infatuation (Aesop 76, Babrius 32).[16]

The disastrous wedding imagines sexual desire undone by another desire more basic and more necessary to the creature who has entered into the marriage. While the goddess of love is able to transform the cat into what she is not for a while, the truth will out. As Babrius puts it, "Desire, having played his game, took his leave: he was worsted by nature" (32.15–16).[17] As is typical in such stories, the animal bride reveals herself through some action characteristic of the animal at a moment of maximum social embarrassment for her husband, in this case the wedding feast itself. The humiliation of having fallen in love with an animal is staged as a public event that dramatizes the cognitive failings induced by an excess of prenuptial desire. Sudden revelation reimagines the waning of attraction in the course of a marriage's growing acquaintance with the object of desire as a single catastrophic event that ends it before it has begun.

---

15. The animal bride story is folktale type 402 in the Aarne-Thompson classification system; see Uther (2004, 1.234–39), and http://www.pitt.edu/~dash/type0402.html.

16. Morgan (2005, 78) refers to the Aesopic tale in a nuanced reading of Semonides' poem within the traditions of ancient wisdom literature and their use of animal fable. Kakridis (1962) compares Semonides' poem to modern Greek animal bride stories in which a father has only one daughter to marry to a large number of men, but is rescued from his embarrassment by divine intervention: the requisite number of brides is made up with animals, and these account for the diversity of women in the present day.

17. In the moralizing Aesopic version of the tale, the conclusion is that "whoever is bad by nature [φύσει] cannot change his ways [τρόπον] even if he changes his shape [φύσιν]," but such moralizing tags obscure the continuity of the animal bride story with the much larger genre of folktales that explore the problem of love between human beings and other forms of life that are partially human in body or soul—mermaids, silkies, and even the incubus I heard about in the Peruvian Amazon: the soul of a drowned gringo that emerges at night from the body of the pink Amazon river dolphin to sleep with indigenous women, a version of the dolphin as white man myth that I learned with some dismay is not recorded in Slater (1994, 202–32); it was told to me on the prow of a speeding motorboat.

Despite the part played by peer observation and the comedy of embarrassment, this is, however, exactly what does not happen in Semonides'
poem. Each man remains married to his animal bride, even though he, and
everyone else, can see what she really is. However different these wives turn
out to be from the brides their husbands had imagined, perception of their
animal natures does not end the marriages into which they entered. In addition, other than a fleeting mention in connection with the bee woman, children and relatives do not appear in the poem. Progeny, and the perpetuation
of family, have no part in its account of marital union. Despite appearances to
the contrary, the female difference the poem imagines as nonhumanness must
be understood to involve some ongoing reenchantment of the appetitive bond
between the married couple—just the opposite of its function in standard versions of the animal bride story.

If, then, Semonides' poem is an extended catalogue of the ways in which
the female member of the human pair is not symmetrical with the male
because she, unlike him, is not entirely human, it is one that argues that the
irreducibility of human life to a single all-encompassing idea of the human
is what, in the end, makes it livable. The poem is well aware that its animal
stories are an investment of imaginative energy in the marriage bond, and it
leaves its readers to imagine what the other side might come up with in the
erotic tales (ἀφροδισίους λόγους; 91), that its women tell one another, and
which so horrify the androcentric bee woman that she cannot bear to be
around them.[18]

The likelihood that there exist complementary narratives giving women's
perceptions of the continuities between their husbands and the males of other
species is signaled here, but not developed. As it is, the poem wraps the bio-
philic fascination with other forms of life that is the engine of cross-species
attraction in simpler animal bride stories with anxieties about the continuities
of behavior between human beings and other animals, even as it points to the
role this mixture of fascination and repulsion plays in securing social bonds.
Indeed, insofar as the poem invokes not only animality but also the elemental
materiality of earth and water as constituents of the wife, it reveals almost too
obviously an intention to fabricate the anxiety-inducing hybrids that Bruno
Latour has argued are the agents of social cohesion in premodern societies—

18. Cf. Osborne, who claims that "the marriage of the disgusting and the desirable is central
to the poem's effect" (2001, 55–59), and that the aim of this marriage in its symposium context
is to re-eroticize the wives who have been left at home in the minds of the husbands who are
participating in it, but understands this eroticization as a lamentably one-sided form of objec-
tification.

our own included—and this disclosure is in keeping with its knowing hint that there is a distaff side to such production.[19]

HUMANS IN ANIMAL PLACES

Animal bride stories present the possibility that animal interiority might take human form and a human being be embarrassed by being discovered experiencing desire for what is only apparently human. As Stanley Cavell has argued, fairy tales of this kind imagine a form of epistemological anxiety as radical as that involved in philosophical skepticism about the existence of the material world, and one of the ways in which they do so is by positing various sorts of superior being capable of revealing human beings' errors to them as they see fit.[20] In Semonides' poem, three sets of observers occupy this elevated position: Zeus and the other Olympians, who made women for men in the way the poem describes, but whose attitudes toward the resulting partnerships are never disclosed; society, imagined as a kind of superorganism that monitors and records the actions of its members more effectively than they can themselves; and the poet, who partakes in both of these positions partially insofar as he can tell his readers what the gods have wrought, if not their reasons for doing it, and reveal operations of the social organism that are hidden to its individual members.[21]

Semonides' poem is not simply an epistemological allegory, nor is it a generalized lament for human beings living under a divine dispensation they do not fully understand. While a universal condition applies, the catalogue mode imagines what it is like to live under it as a set of particular instances: it is one thing to have a slovenly wife whose nature is continuous with that of a pig, quite another to have one whose passivity is continuous with that of an ass. The poem's omniscience is thus both an exemption from the cognitive limitations that afflict ordinary mortals and an understanding of what it feels like to live as the various forms of nonhuman life with which they cohabit. The reve-

---

19. Latour (1993, 112). Cf. Gilhus (2006, 72) on accounts of cross-species love between human beings and other animals in antiquity; here there is no such doubling of hybrids, and hence no similar disclosure of the author's understanding of the work of hybridization itself.

20. Cavell 1979, 416.

21. Cf. Wilson on ant society: "No communal center directs the colony. The social master plan is partitioned into the brains of the all-female workers, whose separate programs fit together to form a balanced whole. Each ant automatically performs certain tasks and avoids others according to its size and age. The superorganism's brain is the entire society" (1984, 36).

lations of ontological difference the poem brings to its readers are ancient history to the husbands of its own narratives, knowledge that they, like everyone else, has lived with since the days of Paris and Helen. What makes the poem more than a display of open secrets is its willingness to interrogate the forms of desire and aversion that have led human beings to posit a belief that beings other than themselves have made their most intimate moments an encounter between one kind of life and another.

In this respect, Semonides' imaginative ambitions are of a piece with Ovid's efforts in the *Metamorphoses* to imagine how human somatic experience might suddenly be transformed by nonhuman agents capable of turning the human body into an animal, a plant, or a stone. It has been claimed that metamorphosis itself is of secondary interest and importance in the poem, merely a vehicle to get to certain stories,[22] or best approached as a trope for its poetics.[23] I want instead to focus on the fictional events themselves: Io, for example, is after all a woman who turns into a cow, allowing Ovid to explore cognitive and affective possibilities that are not available in fictions that limit themselves to purely human subjects. I begin, however, with an episode that features a form of life that is hybrid by nature not by transformation.

In Book 12, Nestor tells the story of the battle between centaurs and the legendary human clan of the Lapiths that took place at the wedding of Pirithous. Drunk with wine, Eurytus, one of the centaurs, tries to haul away the bride, and a fight breaks out. Tables, altars, and dining utensils fly as both sides grab anything that is not nailed down and hurl it at each other. Ovid himself leaves no stone unturned in his effort to imagine the many and various ways in which such unusual creatures might perish, before all of a sudden breaking off, in the midst of this prodigious slaughter, to tell us about the love affair between Cyllarus and Hylonome, two particularly attractive members of the centaur kind:

> multae illum petiere sua de gente, sed una
> abstulit Hylonome, qua nulla decentior inter
> semiferos altis habitavit femina silvis;
> haec et blanditiis et amando et amare fatendo
> Cyllaron una tenet, cultu quoque, quantus in illis

22. Fränkel 1945, 80; Galinsky 1975, 43; Fantham 2004, 14–16.

23. A common theme of the essays in Hardie, Barchiesi, and Hinds (1999); see Farrell (1999, 137); Theodorakopoulos (1999, 142); Gildenhard and Zissos (1999, 162). Feldherr (2002, 164) neatly sums up this tendency in recent criticism of the poem, and points to some of what it misses.

esse potest membris, ut sit coma pectine levis,
ut modo rore maris, modo se violave rosave
implicet, interdum candentia lilia gestet,
bisque die lapsis Pagasaeae vertice silvae
fontibus ora lavet, bis flumine corpora tingat,
nec nisi quae deceant electarumque ferarum
aut umero aut lateri praetendat vellera laevo. (12.404–15)

[Many of the female centaurs sought him, but only one got him, Hylonome, for no more attractive female lived among the half-wild creatures
of the woods. She kept Cyllarus to herself by her charms, by loving,
by confessing that she loved, and by her self-adornment too, insofar as
such a thing is possible with limbs like hers, for she would brush her
lovely hair with a comb, and weave rosemary, violets and roses into it,
or even lilies for special effect. Twice a day she washed her face in the
stream that rushes down from the heights of the Pagasean woods, twice
a day she dipped her body in its waters, and, among the skins of the
carefully chosen wild animals she wore on her shoulder and left side,
there were never any that didn't suit her.]

Passages like this give all the ammunition they need to critics scandal-
ized by Ovid's apparent lack of interest in modeling emotion seriously. Why
would the poet shun the opportunities for pathos afforded by the interjection
of a love story in the midst of a battle narrative and give us this instead?[24] The
description of Hylonome's (Woodwalker's) self-beautification begins inno-
cently enough. It is not so difficult, and even rather touching, to imagine a
half-human, half-equine creature doing her hair and even adorning it with
flowers; there are, as we have seen, long-standing associations between the
beauty of horses and the beauty of women. Likewise, as we follow her to the
stream and watch her bathe, we are easily involved in the erotic whimsy; it is

---

24. Galinsky calls the battle "ludicrous and sensational," and deplores the "cliché-ridden
triteness" and "ludicrous tone" of the story of Cyllarus and Hylonome; both lack "any true
inner dimension" (1975, 117–27, 131). Such complaints are as old as Ovid's ancient readers; see
Seneca *Natural Questions* 3.27.13–15, on his "puerile stupidities," and Dryden's observation,
in the Preface to his *Fables*, that the poet "destroys what he is building," cited in Tissol (1997,
94), who endeavors to rescue Ovid's wit from the readerly desire for familiar human sentiment
that finds fault with it. For Seneca, an index of Ovid's childishness is that he is as interested in
the animals swept up in the great flood of Book 1 as he is in its human victims: the flood scene
"would be magnificent," Seneca claims, if Ovid "had not bothered with what the sheep and the
wolves were doing."

only with the information that Hylonome has a wardrobe of animal skins that we are roused from it. At this point, we realize that the word we had taken to mean something like "self-adornment," *cultus*, in fact indicates something more like "fashion sense."

The passage embeds a structure of readerly disappointment, not to say abuse, and it is only natural to turn this frustration back on the poet as high-minded disapproval. But it only takes a little more reflection to realize how solipsistic and self-indulgent such disappointment really is. We are annoyed with Ovid because he has not given us the feelings to which we think we are entitled and are unhappy that the inner life of a product of his imagination is not what we think it ought to be. So that we can now ask, what was it we assumed as we watched Hylonome's dappled hide glide through the ripples of the mountain stream? Why do we think she shouldn't have the taste of a cultivated shopper? This is the real challenge of Ovid's style: its easy pictorialism invites projection, only to reveal such projections as laughably ill-founded.

The Hylonome episode stages an extreme contrast between actual inner experience and what we are tempted to conclude from the body in which it takes place.[25] Such contrasts appear in many episodes of the poem, with different affective coloring in each. Daphne's lovely body "repels" [*repugnat*] (1.489), the virginity on which her heart is set; Erysichthon is not hungry but has a demon inside him that has colonized his body and is using it to feed (8.790); Glaucus cannot articulate what he feels as a sea creature when he ceases to be one (13.944). Each of these episodes imagines what it would be like to have a body that did not match its possessor's understanding of who he or she is as a person. Each envisages the possibility that having such a body might challenge and even overcome one's ability to be the person one wishes.

For Daphne, for Erysichthon, and for Glaucus, the body presents a different kind of threat to the person that inhabits it, and for each of them the outcome of their struggle with it is different. Daphne's beauty can still be discerned in the laurel tree she becomes; Erysichthon dies by eating himself; Glaucus lives a double life. Their stories are complemented by those in which a singular human identity is sustained and recognized in the nonhuman, and even nonanimal, body it comes to inhabit. Again, the affective tone is varied: Lycaon as wolf is the "image of ferocity" (1.236) he was as a man; the river god

---

25. Cf. Wollheim (1984, 6–7) who argues that our disappointed assumptions about the interiority of nonhuman beings reveal a speciesism the poem intends to test.

Alpheus recognizes Arethusa, the woman he desired, in the "beloved waters" she has become (5.636); Cadmus as a snake licks the face of his beloved wife (4.595). She wishes for a body like his, and they are able to continue their married life as "gentle serpents," mindful of what they were before (4.603).

In these episodes, an animating human consciousness is able to use a non-human body to signal its presence to another human being. Perhaps this is because it operates its new form badly and reveals itself as one form of life poorly concealed in the guise of another, like a comic actor in the costume of a bird. For when the gods disguise themselves, their transformations typically go unrecognized. Some women feel, or understand, their presence in an animal that makes love to them, as golden-haired Ceres "knew" [*sensit*] Poseidon as a horse, Medusa knew him as a bird, and Melantho as a dolphin (6.118–20), but others are simply deceived, and experience the bestial form as pure imposition, as when Jupiter tricked the daughter of Deo as a snake (6.114).

Mortal partners in divine love may be denied the pleasure of recognizing and acknowledging the god in his altered form, but what they don't know doesn't hurt them, unlike the many failed recognition scenes in which such ignorance either comes close to, or actually ends in, disaster. So Philemon and Baucis alone are spared the punishment that is visited upon their neighbors for not revering gods that walk the earth in human form (8.627), the sailors who fail to recognize Bacchus are turned into dolphins (3.670), and Pentheus is torn apart by his family, who think he is a boar (3.714). Only divine intervention saves Callisto as a bear from being killed by her own son, whose response to the uncanny look in her animal eyes is terrified aggression:

> incidit in matrem, quae restitit Arcade viso
> et cognoscenti similis fuit: ille refugit
> inmotosque oculos in se sine fine tenentem
> nescius extimuit propiusque accedere aventi
> vulnifico fuerat fixurus pectora telo. (2.500–4)

[He came upon his mother, who stopped still when Arcas appeared and looked like someone with understanding. He drew back and, without knowing why, feared what kept its unmoving eyes upon him. As it tried to come closer, he prepared to fix his wound-bringing spear in its breast.]

Arcas finds something in the eyes of a hunted animal that he has not seen there before, a look of recognition that, without his knowing why, triggers a fearful desire to kill what has not offered to harm him. The discourse of the eyes testifies to the presence of something humanlike inside the bear that disconfirms what Arcas is accustomed to believe about such animals. Io's family likewise do not know what it is (*ignorant quae sit*) when they meet the friendly cow she has become (1.642). Her name is simple enough that she can spell it out with her hoof, but she is an exception. The list of characters who struggle unsuccessfully to speak as animals, and cannot make themselves known in any other way, is lengthy.[26]

Ovid rarely imagines transformation into an animal as gaining a power human beings do not possess, such as flight. Only gods enjoy their metamorphoses, presumably because they can change back at will.[27] Human beings given animal form do not understand what it is like to be the animal they have become: Callisto as a bear is still afraid of wild animals, including other bears (2.493–95). What they and those who encounter them do gain is a new understanding of their limitations, the knowledge that human beings are subject to divine fiats they cannot anticipate or control, and that what they are given to inhabit in any form is an animal body with certain capabilities and not others.

Ovid's transformed persons suffer impairments no divinity can know, and, in the chastening experiential corrections to which they are subjected, they are found to be much closer to animals than gods. Book 1 contains a brief hand-me-down account of human beings' natural dominion over the animals, for which they are equipped by their superior minds and upright posture. What follows, however, is a statement of their doubtful origins that imagines being human as a condition of ongoing ontological anxiety: human beings came into existence after the animals, but it is unknown whether they were made by a god from his own substance, or whether Prometheus scooped up some leftovers of the sky that were mingled with the earth, and somehow molded them into an image, or effigy, of the gods (1.76–88).

This passage speaks of a kind of homelessness in the world on the part of human beings, separated from the animals by their later birth and peculiar stance, but unsure of their kinship with higher beings. Every transformation in the poem underlines the futility of their efforts to close the gap between themselves and the gods by widening the one between themselves and the

26. Io 1.731–33, Clymene 2.333, Chariclo 2.665, Actaeon 3.192–203, Cadmus 4.588–89, the Pierides 5.695, Alcyone 11.731, the Cecropians 14.91, Macareus 14.277, Acmon 14.497.

27. So Mercury flies like a kite (2.708), and Jupiter makes a handsome bull (2.846); cf. Riddehough (1959, 204).

animals.[28] In Book 15, however, Ovid imagines a long speech by Pythagoras that attempts instead to close the gap between human beings and animals and put an end to the epistemological and ontological doubts that plague human life with the doctrine of metempsychosis: the spirit that in one life animates a human body may occupy the body of a nonhuman animal in another, and human beings should not eat other animals because their bodies may contain "familiar souls" [*cognatas animas*] (15.165).

The ontological claim provides a straightforward answer to the cognitive questions raised by animal behavior and expression. To Pythagoras, the sound of a young goat at the slaughter is like the wailing of a human child, and only an impious person can hear it with "unmoved ears" (15.465). For the sage, the failure of human beings to grasp what animals are trying to tell them that we have witnessed elsewhere in the poem is willful inattention on their part. Animals voice their feelings and their preferences clearly; human beings simply choose not to heed them when they pursue pleasures that cost them their lives. Pythagoras reframes possibilities that in the rest of the poem appear as fantastic and singular events from the prehistory of human culture as issues involved in its most everyday practices. However, what his speech gains in the way of pragmatic cultural criticism, it loses in imaginative intensity. As philosophical discourse, it does not have the resources of poetic narrative at its disposal in its efforts to reorient human behavior toward killing and eating. The philosopher can tell us what the life of animals is like, but only the poet can make us feel it for ourselves.[29]

As I have argued already, Ovid seldom approaches this task directly by giving us a sympathetic account of what it would be like to acquire the capabilities of another animal. His is a *via negativa* of the imagination: we grasp what it would feel like to have a different body by grasping what it would feel like to be incapable of doing something we do automatically with our own. So when Juno sends Argus to keep an eye on Io as a cow, Io tries unsuccessfully to make contact with her guardian and elicit his pity for her:

> illa etiam supplex Argo cum bracchia vellet
> tendere, non habuit, quae bracchia tenderet Argo,
> et conata queri mugitus edidit ore

28. Cf. Fränkel (1945, 162–63), who imagines Ovid as a poet stranded between pagan antiquity and Christianity, and the comments on his tragic Ovid in Hardie (2002, 27–28).

29. Cf. Galinsky (1998), who, partly in response to Hardie (1995), sees an agonistic relationship to the philosophical tradition in Ovid's inclusion in his poem of a Pythagoras divested of serious intellectual purpose.

pertimuitque sonos propriaque exterrita voce est.
venit et ad ripas, ubi ludere saepe solebat,
Inachidas ripas, novaque ut conspexit in unda
cornua, pertimuit seque exsternata refugit. (1.635–41)

[When she wanted to stretch out her arms to Argus as a suppliant, she had no arms that she could stretch out to Argus, and when she tried to complain she brought forth moos from her mouth; she was frightened by the sounds and terrified at her own voice. She went to the riverbanks where she used to play, which were those of her father Inachus, but when she saw her new horns in the water she was frightened, and shrank back terrified from herself.]

Io's efforts to use her body combine the agonizing repetition of the phantom limb experience, in which a person tries—and cannot stop himself from trying—to use a body part that is no longer there, with the frustration and discomfort of learning how to work its artificial prosthesis. Once again, Ovid's wit is intrusive and excruciating; the first two lines reproduce Io's plight as a knockabout syntactical comedy in which the clumsy doubling of "stretch arms" mimes the incapacity that results from the replacement of arms by an extra pair of legs. Yet the clowning that reproduces physical lack as verbal excess has a sympathetic, and even a philosophical, point: it is by watching someone who is unable to operate a body that we come to understand that bodies are not things we operate, however natural it may be to think so.[30]

Only gods can "use" bodies, because only gods do not require a particular physical instantiation to be themselves.[31] What else can Io's fear of herself mean? She cannot be afraid of her horns because she is afraid of injuring herself with them—she would be unable to do so even if she wanted to; she is afraid because these are now her body. But why fear, rather than, say, horror or disgust, which one might think would be more obvious emotions in her situation? When Actaeon, the hunter who stumbles upon the goddess Diana as she is bathing in the woods, is transformed into a deer, he is given the affects of a deer, but there is no such suggestion here and no reason to think that a cow would be frightened of its own reflection in any case. Io's fear

---

30. Cf. Wollheim: "Whole areas that we can make sense of only when they are the province of spontaneity become, we have now to believe, regulated by trial and error" (1984, 7).

31. Hardie (2002, 169–70) contrasts Dionysus, who can be both human being and animal, with Actaeon, who cannot combine, or choose between, these possibilities.

is a human response to her situation. We see her from the outside as she performs the movements and makes the sounds of the cow she has become, and
until she hits on the idea of writing her name, no one suspects that she is not
one. Can it be that for a moment she believes it too?

Io's transformation imagines that with memories, intentions, and emotions
intact, it would nonetheless be possible to believe that one was no longer a
human being. Nothing in Io's consciousness of herself suggests this possibility to her before she sees her reflection, and in this she differs from Actaeon,
whose transformation into a stag is accompanied by changes in self-awareness
that preclude any such surprise. Animals' incapacity for human speech, which
so often torments transformed human beings, is, in this episode, an explicit
motive for the transformation; Diana changes Actaeon into an animal so that
he will not be able to report what he has seen: "Now you may tell that you
have seen me without my clothes—if you are able to tell it, that is."

Ovid enjoys Diana's ironic sense of her own power. He calls her transformation of Actaeon a gift; she gives him (*dat*) the horns of stag; gives him
a long neck, pointed ears, feet for hands, and legs for arms; and "clothes" or
"drapes" (*velat*) his body with a speckled hide. Finally, Ovid tells us, fear is
added to Actaeon (*additus et pavor est*) so that "the hero, son of Autonoe,"
runs away. As Actaeon flees, he "wonders at himself, that he should be so
swift in flight"; he no longer knows who he is now that his limbs react to fear
without his being able to control them. If comparison makes any sense in
such contexts, Actaeon's transformation is more horrifying than Io's because
Diana does not simply alter his body but modifies the subjectivity around
which any body, even an animal body, ought to form an impermeable border.
Most alarmingly of all, perhaps, the passive verb suggests that Diana does not
simply implant fear in Actaeon but that her initial gift of an animal body by
itself produces a new set of effects inside it. When Actaeon sees what he has
become by virtue of this addition, his reaction is pity, not fear: he understands
that, while his mind is what it was, the person of which that mind had been
one part no longer exists:

> ut vero vultus et cornua vidit in unda,
> "me miserum!" dicturus erat: vox nulla secuta est;
> ingemuit: vox illa fuit, lacrimaeque per ora
> non sua fluxerunt; mens tantum pristina mansit. (3.200–3)

[When he saw his features and his horns in the water he was about to say
"Poor me!" but no voice followed. He groaned: that was his voice, and

tears flowed down the face that was not his; his mind alone remained as it had been.]

As Actaeon pauses to drink, he is torn between returning home to face his family and remaining in the woods to hide. Shame contends with fear, human emotion with animal affect, and the outcome of the conflict is blockage and death: as he stands rooted to the spot in perplexity, he is spotted by his hounds who give chase. Between the dogs' sighting of their master and their pursuit of him, however, there intervenes one of the strangest moments in a poem full of strange and fantastic events: Ovid suspends the flow of the story and gives us a nineteen-line catalogue of the dogs' names. Beginning with Melampus and Ichnobates (Blackfoot and Trailhunter), he lists thirty of them, until we get to Argiodus and Hylactor (Whitetooth and Woodrunner), whereupon he informs us, in a kind of narrative footnote, that there were actually more, but these would be "tedious to relate" (3.206–225).

It is an impressive metrical *tour de force* to fit thirty or so Greek names into half as many lines of Latin verse, but why has Ovid given us this triumph of technical facility instead of human sympathy? In addition to the dogs' names, we are told their geographical origins, their pedigree, and details of their body and temperament. Is the poet individualizing, or even humanizing, the dogs, as animals that belong to a human household, in contrast to the wild animal their master has become? But this is not how they act. For Ovid, with a word typically used for agglomerations of human beings, presents their behavior as that of a pack, an animal group animated by a single desire: "Over cliffs and peaks and rocks that are difficult of access, where the way is difficult and where is none at all, in their lust for prey that crowd pursue him" [*ea turba . . . sequuntur*] (3.225–27).

The catalogue that throws us off our hunt for pathos is the means by which Ovid shifts the episode's affective center from Actaeon's self-pity to the orgiastic bloodlust of his dogs. If we didn't get it the first time, the structure is repeated in miniature in the lines that follow. Ovid introduces another three hounds by name—Melanchaetes, Theridamas, and Oresitrophus (Blackcoat, Beastslayer and Mountainbred)—and, as these cut off their master's escape, the rest leap on him *en masse*: "The remainder of the pack gathers, and their teeth meet in his body" [*cetera turba coit confertque in corpore dentes*]. This is the poem's most brutal deterritorialization. As Actaeon's cries fill the hills he knows so well, his body becomes a site in which his hounds' teeth converge, until, as they tear him to pieces, there is "no place left for wounds" (3.236–37).

As Actaeon is killed, he sinks to his knees like a person begging for mercy, and "casts silent looks around as if they were his arms" [*circumfert tacitos tamquam sua bracchia vultus*] (3.241). The discourse of the eyes is always liable to go unheard, and, when Actaeon's fellow hunters catch up with him, they, like his dogs, fail to identify him. They continue to call upon him "as if he were absent," and Ovid gives us a variation on the misrecognition scene whose verbal high jinks encapsulate the difficulty of responding to his poem as a whole:

ad nomen caput ille refert et abesse queruntur
nec capere oblatae segnem spectacula praedae.
vellet abesse quidem, sed adest. (3.245-47)

[Actaeon turns his head towards his name and his friends complain that he is not there and that because of his sluggishness he is missing the spectacle of the prey that has presented itself. He might well want not to be there, but he is there.]

Actaeon's friends complain that he is not there (*abesse*); Actaeon himself wishes he wasn't there (*abesse*), but there he is, after all (*adest*). This is the "wit out of season" that Dryden complained of in the *Heroides*: like Actaeon the deer, something is present that ought to be absent, and something is absent that ought to be present. Ovid imagines a situation of maximum physical and emotional duress for Actaeon and denies him and us the opportunity to experience it humanly. His death frustrates readers looking for the comforts of literary emotion, the kind they are accustomed to in books of human suffering.[32]

HUNTING, KILLING, TALKING

Ovid's characters endure immensities of suffering; their world contains agents whose power exceeds anything they could have imagined before their

32. Cf. Deleuze and Guattari on how Kafka wept with laughter at situations over which his critics have shed tears of pity: "Only one thing really bothers Kafka and angers him, makes him indignant: when people treat him as a writer of intimacy, finding a refuge in literature, as an author of solitude, of guilt, of an intimate misfortune . . . There is a Kafka laughter, a very joyous laughter, that people usually understand poorly . . . He is an author who laughs with a profound joy, a *joie de vivre*, in spite of, or because of, his clownish declarations that he offers like a trap or a circus" (1986, 41).

transformative encounter with them. The poet's aggressive narration, which inflicts spectacular metamorphoses on his characters and denies his readers the pleasures they want to feel in response to them, enacts the experience of divinity, from whose perspective human life and human death is, as Wordsworth saw it, an affectless spectacle, bodies "rolled round in earth's diurnal course,│With rocks, and stones, and trees."[33]

The possibility that Diana's ironic attitude toward Actaeon's death indicates incomprehension of what it is that her mortal victim is about to undergo locates the episode in both the ancient traditions of metamorphic poetry and the ancient traditions of hunting poetry, in which the capacity of different kinds of beings to comprehend death is a constant theme. Indeed, it was believed in antiquity that Ovid's last work was a poem on sea fishing, the *Halieutica*, now generally considered spurious, whose surviving lines offer a remarkable reflection on the relationship between defensive behavior and mental representation in animals threatened with harm:

Accepit mundus legem: dedit arma per omnes
admonuitque sui: vitulus sic namque minatur,
qui nondum gerit in tenera iam cornua fronte;
sic dammae fugiunt, pugnant virtute leones
et morsu canis, et caudae sic scorpios ictu,
concussique levis pinnis sic evolat ales.
Omnibus ignotae mortis timor, omnibus hostem
praesidiumque datum sentire et noscere teli
vimque modumque sui. (1–9)

[The universe adopted a law: it [or a god] gave arms to all creatures and instructed them in their use:[34] thus the calf already threatens when it does not yet bear horns on its tender forehead, thus does flee, lions fight with their courage, the dog with its bite, and the scorpion with the blow

33. Wordsworth (1904, 149). My understanding of Ovid's aggression is informed by Malouf (1978, 153–54), in which the novelist takes the poet to task for not taking his imagination more seriously, and asserts that the intention of his own book is "to make this glib fabulist of 'the changes' live out in reality what had been, in his previous existence, merely the occasion for dazzling literary display."

34. These lines are obscure because what precedes them has been lost. I have preferred the text and interpretation of Capponi (1972), with which Saint-Denis (1975) substantially agrees, to that of Richmond (1962), although I have profited from his interpretation of the passage as a whole.

of its tail, while the light bird flies away on agitated wings. In all there is
a fear of death, of which they know nothing, to all is given knowledge of
their enemies, and watchfulness against them, with an understanding of
the strength and limitations of their own weapons.]

As this poem imagines it, animals have a practical understanding of how to
make best use of their defensive capabilities. It is a physiological endowment
that manifests itself as instinctual behavior before they are involved in situations in which they will have to make use of their powers in earnest. Their
understanding falls short of a full grasp of such situations, however, because
animals lack a concept of death, even though their bodies and behavior are
designed to avoid it. If attempts upon their lives do not take the form of overt
hostility that triggers the defensive behavior with which nature has equipped
them to respond to it, they do not understand that they are in life-threatening
situations because, unlike human beings, they do not live with the consciousness of death as the end of life.[35]

The belief that only human beings know death and animals merely respond
to threats is not so much explicitly challenged in the *Metamorphoses* as it is
bracketed by episodes that draw parallels between gods, human beings, and
animals, in their experience of both: Pythagoras observes that the sound of a
young goat at the slaughter resembles the cries of a human child (15.463–68);
Apollo groans at the infidelity of his lover Coronis "no differently than when
a hammer, with a clear blow delivered beside the right ear, smashes apart the
hollow temples of a nursing calf as the cow looks on" (2.623–25); Itys calls out
"Mother! Mother!" (6.640) as Procne is about to cut his throat like a sacrificial animal.

Analogy becomes explicit argument in the *Cynegetica*, a Greek poem about
hunting attributed to Oppian but dedicated to the emperor Caracalla, and
therefore unlikely to be the work of the same Oppian who wrote a *Halieutica* dedicated to Marcus Aurelius that enjoyed wide appeal.[36] For the author

35. So Pythagoras claims that sacrificial animals do not grasp the import of the knife with
which they are to be killed (*Metamorphoses* 15.132–35), and Seneca, cited by all three commentators on *Halieutica* 7, asserts that animals have an innate knowledge of what will harm them,
not one that is acquired by experience (*Letter* 121.19).

36. Whitby suggests that the "Callimachean aesthetics and proportions" of the *Halieutica*, of which there are seventy-one surviving manuscripts, explains its popularity, whereas the
"rhetorical mannerisms and lexical novelties" of the *Cynegetica*, of which there are nineteen
surviving manuscripts, proved less appealing (2007, 125–26). What one would like to know,
however, is why the insistent pathos of animal death in both poems did not offend the sensibili-

of the *Cynegetica* appears to be less interested in how to catch animals than in dramatizing the suffering they endure in being hunted in such a way as to suggest the continuity of their mental representations with those of human beings. So, when he comes to the hunting of wild goats, for example, he imagines the defensive behavior of a mother goat toward her children to include explicit articulation of the death that threatens them:

τὴν μὲν γὰρ δοκέοις παῖδας μύθοισι δίεσθαι,
λισσομένην τοίοισιν ἀπόπροθι μηκηθμοῖσι·
φεύγετέ μοι, φίλα τέκνα, δυσαντέας ἀγρευτῆρας,
μή με λυγρὴν δμηθέντες ἀμήτορα μητέρα θῆτε.
τοῖα φάμεν δοκέοις. (2.358–61)

[You would think she was chasing away her children with words, begging them to go far away with her bleating: "Flee from the cruel huntsmen, my dear children, lest by killing you they make me a grieving mother who is a mother no more." This is what you would think she said.]

The passage turns the resemblance between the cries of animals and human speech in Pythagoras's account of animal sacrifice into a fully realized dramatic situation. The poet puts us on the spot and tells us that, were we there, we would hear in the mother goat's voice not just an approximation of the cries of a human infant, but discretely articulated units of utterance like those of adult human speech. The real genius is in the sound: the mother goat's address to her children is made up of *m*'s and long *e*'s that not only compose human words but also reproduce the sound of bleating that is captured onomatopoeically in *mêkêthmos*, the Greek noun for goat noise that introduces her utterance: *mê me lugrên dmêthentes amêtora mêtera thête*.

Oppian's narrative resembles Aristotle's account of bird song that cannot but strike the observer as an exchange of information, but this imaginative response is here extended to an animal that, on Aristotle's understanding of the physiology of vocal production, is capable only of voice (φωνή), not articulate speech. Here, too, unlike Aristophanes' *Birds*, animal utterance does not weave in and out of human speech, being either one or the other at any given moment, but is rather both at the same time; both, that is to say, a

---

ties of elite readers for whom representations of hunting in the plastic arts were "a symbol of wealth and power" (134).

mimetic representation of the sound of a goat's bleating and a fully intelligible piece of human language.[37]

By framing the mother goat's utterance with the repeated "you would think" [δοκέοις], Oppian invites his readers to consider what would be required on their part to hear it as speech, and what would be involved in refusing it this status. In Sophocles' *Philoctetes*, the tragic hero's distress calls drive away his human companions, undoing the networks of sociality that hold human speakers to their bonds with others. The mother goat's pleas have the opposite effect, drawing her children to her when she wishes they would flee:

> τοὺς δ' ἑσταότας προπάροιθε
> πρῶτα μὲν ἀείδειν στονόεν μέλος ἀμφὶ τεκούσῃ,
> αὐτὰρ ἔπειτ' ἐνέπειν φαίης μεροπήιον ἠχήν,
> ῥηξαμένους βληχήν, στομάτων τ' ἄπο τοῖον ἀυτεῖν,
> φθεγγομένοις ἰκέλους καὶ λισσομένοισιν ὁμοίους (2.362–66)

[Standing before her you would say that they first sang a mournful dirge for their begetter, then spoke the language of mortal men, breaking forth in bleating, and from their mouths uttered such words as this, like human speakers and resembling those who supplicate.]

The young goats perform the parts of a tragedy, singing a mournful song like a chorus, then returning to the urgent task of dialogue with their pursuer. Oppian this time puts his readers on the spot by framing his rendition of the young goats' utterance with verbs that typically introduce visual ecphrasis: "You would say [φαίης] they sang a mournful dirge . . . Such things one would think them to utter as ones who supplicate, [τοῖά τις ἂν δόξειε λιταζομένους ἀγορεύειν]" (2.364–73). The imagined observer, confronted by aural rather than visual phenomena, is asked to take his natural understanding as the guide to a communicational situation in which clear analogies of posture and emotional expressiveness are the ground that allows for comprehension of a message whose obviousness enables its translation into human speech.

37. Cf. Kroodsma: "As babies, too, both male and female alders weakly called *fee-bee-o* when I temporarily moved them from the group and isolated them in the quiet of another room. *Where-are-you?, I-am-here*, they seemed to call in their baby voices" (2005, 84) Here, too, the observer's sense that the young birds feel threatened induces him to hear a particular content in their repeated cry.

But there is more at stake here than human beings' ability to comprehend what other animals are trying to tell them from their vocal utterances. The young goats beg the hunter for their mother's release in the name of the gods, calling upon Zeus and Artemis, imploring him to curb his untamed heart, and respect divine justice. Finally, they ask him to consider whether he too has an aged parent "left behind in his bright home" (2.367–72). The goats' entreaty to the hunter to remember his own begetter recalls Priam's plea to Achilles in Book 24 of the *Iliad*, where the Trojan king's success in asking for the return of his son's body rests upon his ability to convince his fearsome adversary of the analogy between his father's situation and his own. As Oppian sees it, the ability to grasp an animal's affects from its utterances entails the ability to emplot them as an extension of the sympathetic imagination.

As we saw in the introduction, Adam Smith believed that the Greek tragedies that attempted "to excite compassion by the representation of bodily pain" were "among the greatest breaches of decorum of which the Greek theatre has set the example." Smith's examples were "the physical agonies of Hercules and Hippolytus"—Hercules consumed by the pain of the centaur's poisoned shirt at the end of Sophocles' *Women of Trachis*, and Hippolytus torn apart by horses in Euripides' play named after him. Oppian answers Smith's objection to the absence of narrative in mere cries of pain by imagining that the conditions in which the nonverbal utterances that convey tragedy's most intense affects are produced—affects that are continuous with those of the other animals—already contain possibilities for narrative elaboration that can be grasped by their auditor by virtue of his natural understanding. As Priam's words have no power over Achilles until he allows them to be informed by the paternal affects from which they emerge, so the bleating of the goats is imagined both as mere sound and as an entreaty whose actualization requires modes of cognition beyond those of verbal decoding alone. The outcome is never a given, for it depends upon the listener's sympathies: the hunter may be persuaded, but, if he has a heart that is entirely without pity (κραδίην παναμείλιχον), the young goats will follow their mother into bondage (2.374–76).

Oppian's strategy here is, one might argue, the reverse of Ovid's in the Actaeon episode. Rather than telling the story of the goats to its end but withholding the affects to which the reader feels entitled, the poet offers two possible outcomes and asks the reader which would transpire if his own sympathetic understanding were the determining factor. We can get the literary experience we crave, but only if we are willing to accept that nonhuman agents can be the subjects and vehicles of tragic emotion.[38] But Oppian does not merely produce animals as proper subjects of poetic mimesis; he claims that the most exceptionally pathetic scenes of the most exceptionally pathetic poems are inflicted upon them. For in addition to the end of the *Iliad*, animals also relive Sophocles' *Oedipus Rex* in his poem—the best of tragedies by virtue of its exemplary emplotment of ignorance and recognition, according to the *Poetics*. In the *Cynegetica*, the poet tells of a thoroughbred stallion tricked into mating with his mother by an unscrupulous owner who wishes to perpetuate their breed (1.236-70). Disgusted by the discovery of what has been done to them, the horses leap to their deaths from a rocky cliff and perish "leaning their heads on one another," as the "horrible Cadmean marriage of the wandering Oedipus once celebrated among men" is repeated in their lives. Like Sophocles' Apollo, their owner initiates a tragedy he cannot understand.

WE HAVE NEVER BEEN HUMAN

Zoological prose writers from late antiquity have been criticized for recycling material from Aristotle's work on animals for the sake of philosophical polemics without direct observation of their own.[39] The intertextual reenactments in the *Cynegetica*, by contrast, are of such super-canonical moments of epic and tragedy that an edgy sentimentality results from them that cannot help but provoke meta-reflection on analogy itself. In particular, Oppian's use of intertextual analogy does not simply assert continuities of affect between human beings and animals, it also reminds readers that imagination is required if such continuities are to be actualized as sympathetic understanding. We might think that the horses' suffering is like that of Oedipus and Jocasta, just as we might think the mother goat is speaking to her children, but we might refuse the apparent resemblances instead, and even resent being asked to make the leap: analogy may lead to antipathy as well as to sympathy.

So, too, Gilbert White, in *The Natural History of Selborne*, draws attention to the part played by feeling in analogy's power to reorient imaginative understanding. He tells the story of the accidental discovery of a mole cricket's nest: a gardener trimming a walk cuts too deeply with his scythe and lays open to

38. Cf. Bartley (2003, 3–11, 210–11, 302) on Oppian's similes as a way of insisting on the continuities of human life with that of other animals.

39. See French (1994) on Plutarch (178–84), Pliny (218–30), and Aelian (264–66). Russo (2004, 231–42) is even harsher. Prose versions of the horse suicide can be found in Aristotle *History of Animals* 631a; and Aelian *Natural History* 4.7.

view a "curious scene of domestic economy" beneath the turf. Instead, however, of proceeding directly to his description of the burrow filled with the insect's eggs, White cites a passage from Virgil's *Aeneid* that describes the moment in the sack of Troy when Neoptolemus tears the doors off Priam's palace and exposes to view the altars and women's rooms within:

> . . . ingentem lato dedit ore fenestram:
> apparent domus intus, et atria longa patescunt:
> apparent . . . penetralia.

> [He makes a huge window with a gaping mouth: the insides of the house are visible, and the long halls are exposed to view; the inner sancta can be seen.]

> There were caverns and winding passages leading to a kind of chamber, neatly smoothed and rounded, and about the size of a moderate snuffbox. Within this secret nursery were deposited nearly an hundred eggs of a dirty yellow color.[40]

What is it about the juxtaposition of these two scenes that is so disturbing? First, the crickets seem to have technicized the reproductive behavior that, in human beings, is both a source of intimacy and the motive for the architectural technology that gives such intimacy a space in which it can be expressed. Second, this technicization is expressed in the same kind of architecture that human beings employ for intimate space. Third, the differences in the way human beings and crickets have organized their reproductive behavior only partially conceals the similarity in reproductive biology that lies behind them: both animals produce eggs but the mole crickets' are stacked and hatched in a corporate nursery outside the female's body.

White's classical analogy renders the perception that the mole crickets' nest is a solution to the problem of raising offspring in safety analogous to the one human beings have devised as a psychic movement akin to the action of memory. As a memorized poem is brought out of the mental storage where it ordinarily resides, so acknowledgment of biological kinship emerges from the deep place in consciousness to which it has been confined. The crickets recur in Verlyn Klinkenborg's rewriting of *The Natural History* from the perspec-

---

40. White (1977, 230 [Letter XLVIII]). The translation of Virgil is my own; White does not include one.

tive of White's pet tortoise—*Timothy; or, Notes of an Abject Reptile*—where they illustrate a general human tendency to find certain animals instructive, but not others, and the tendency of White, in particular, to prioritize sexual desire as a motivation in other animals, which strikes Timothy as odd in a man of the cloth.[41]

Klinkenborg's book is a masterly example of the postmodern rewrite of a canonical work from the critical perspective of one of its minor characters:[42] Timothy's Archilochean abjection brings a deep attachment to his own embodiment, and the particular affects this embodiment entails, to bear on his master's belief that an animal such as himself must be grateful to his human captors for freeing him from his natural condition (42–43). Timothy, in turn, attributes human beings' inability to see what is actually going on in the lives of the other animals around them to their dependence upon a certain kind of gaze that leaves them incapable of responding to all but a tiny bandwidth in the total spectrum of nonhuman communication:

> Thousands of pairs of eyes in this garden. Few of them able to make a human feel looked at. Strangely impervious to the level gaze of a swallow or a bumble bee. No natural predators. Unaware of the menace in a hedgehog's glare. Blind to the query in a bantam's eye. Few creatures cast their wishes into a look. Those alone catch a human's notice. (74)

As Timothy sees it, human beings' indifference to some animals, like their attachment to others, is a consequence of their having a particular physiology of perception that makes them receptive to certain messages and oblivious to others. There are thresholds of experience proper to them, and they cannot apprehend communication from beyond their circumscribed domain. But has Timothy's understanding not been led astray by his own mode of perception here? The revelation of the mole crickets' nest is sudden and unexpected, and it gives White no opportunity to block out the analogy with human reproductive behavior it provokes in him. So, given that an unguarded moment does allow a discerning response to an animal he would not usually acknowledge, might we not think that some sort of sentinel posted at the doors of percep-

---

41. Klinkenborg (2006, 76, 102).

42. On the phenomenon generally, see Doležel (1998, 199–226). The "Historical Note" with which Klinkenborg's narrative ends—"this is a true story . . . Timothy was indeed female" (159)—also repays comparison with the "Afterword: A Note on Sources," with which Malouf (1978) concludes. For both rewriters, there is a failure of attention and imagination in the protowork that is best corrected by fictionalizing supplementation.

tion, rather than incapacity, is the cause of White's typically human inability to respond to such indications of kinship under ordinary circumstances?

Compare Neil Shubin's *Your Inner Fish*, "a journey into the 3.5-billion-year history of the human body," that promises to teach its readers how "our hands actually resemble fish fins, and major parts of our genome look, and function, like those of worms and bacteria." On the cover, Oliver Sacks explains that the book "will change forever how you understand what it means to be human," and a full-color flap entitled "Your Body as You've Never Seen It Before" that appears between the cover and first page proclaims the joys of evolutionary knowledge: "learn to LOVE your body for what it really is: a jury-rigged fish," says *Discover* magazine. "A DELIGHTFUL introduction to our skeletal structure, viscera, and other vital parts," the *Los Angeles Times* agrees.[43] Can one experience one's body in a way that is cognizant of its deep historical continuity with the physiology of fish, and, if so, would such knowledge take the form of love?

Ovid, in Book 13 of the *Metamorphoses*, tells the story of Glaucus, who, nibbling one day on an unknown herb growing by the edge of the sea, finds "his lower organs suddenly trembling inside him," and "his chest seized with love of another nature." Unable to control himself, he leaps into the ocean, and before long finds himself among sea gods who take away his mortal—or human—elements. Rivers flow in upon him from all sides, and he loses consciousness of his experiences:

> hactenus acta tibi possum memoranda referre,
> hactenus et memini, nec mens mea cetera sensit. (13.955–56)

> [To this point I can tell you what it was that I did, to this point I remember things, but of the rest my mind retains no trace.]

When he returns from his underwater sojourn, Glaucus finds himself "alien in all of [his] body from what [he] had been before" (13.958–59), and he takes in this altered person with a consciousness that is itself no longer what it had been prior to his immersion. His green beard and the long mane that trails the ocean's surface like the arms of a jellyfish, the huge shoulders

43. "LOVE" and "DELIGHTFUL" were presumably reset in capital letters with eye-catching shadows by Shubin's publisher, but the analogy to shoddy mechanical retrofitting is the author's own. He compares the human body to a poorly renovated building (86) and a Volkswagen Beetle with after-market modifications (185): the human brain stem evolved to control breathing in fish, and has been "jury-rigged to work in mammals" (191).

and blue limbs of an aquatic creature, do not intimidate him, for the mind that would have been frightened by such an appearance has been left behind in the depths of the sea: he contemplates a body that is like the bodies of fish with thoughts that are no longer human. As a result, he neither loves nor hates his new body, but merely accepts it as his own. He literally feels nothing for his transformation, and is hurt only by his repulse at the hands of the still lovely Scylla, who is not yet the barking sea dog she will become.

Because Glaucus cannot remember how he got to be the way he is he does not live out his metamorphosis as a painful loss of humanness, but contemplates his fishhood with unparalleled equanimity. Not so the narrator of H. P. Lovecraft's "The Shadow Over Innsmouth." This story, in which a cult of the Phoenician fish god Dagon is imported into an obscure section of the New England coast, is clearly informed by evolutionary theory. The town drunk, who relates the subservience of Innsmouth's inhabitants to the sea gods who have taken up residence among them, informs the narrator that "human folks has got a kind o' relation to sech water-beasts," because "everything alive come aout o' the water onct," and the story tracks its teller's changing feelings toward his own belief that acknowledging this relation means devolving from humanness and becoming a fish again.[44]

The narrator, an amateur antiquarian, undertakes the difficult journey to Innsmouth because he is intrigued by a piece of jewelry from there that has made its way into a museum in a neighboring town against the wishes of its rightful owners. Its oceanic imagery provokes a mixture of fascination and repulsion in him that seems to draw upon deep physiological memories of its animal forms:

> The patterns all hinted of remote secrets and unimaginable abysses in time and space, and the monotonously aquatic nature of the reliefs became almost sinister. Among these reliefs were fabulous monsters of abhorrent grotesqueness and malignity—half ichthyic and batrachian in suggestion—which one could not dissociate from a certain haunting and uncomfortable sense of pseudo-memory, as if they called up some image from deep cells and tissues whose retentive functions are wholly primal and awesomely ancestral. (595–96)

At this point, the narrator's attitude is manifestly defensive. He calls what his body knows "pseudo-memory," preferring to believe that it does not dis-

44. Lovecraft 2005, 616.

close the truth of his being but functions instead as a kind of fiction-making machine, projecting delusions up into his mind where they can be censored and rejected.[45] When he sees the actual inhabitants of Innsmouth, however, they "start up vestigial fears and aversions that not even the stoutest philosophy can disperse" (608). He endeavors to steady himself against the "shuddering touch of evil pseudo-memory," but his bodily apprehensions turn out to have been right all along: the town really is peopled by recidivist beings who, some time toward middle age, begin to show signs of their piscine ancestry before taking to the ocean once and for all.

After barely escaping from Innsmouth with his life, Lovecraft's narrator discovers through genealogical researches that his own ancestors are from the town and that this knowledge has previously been concealed from him. He now experiences the onset of metamorphosis in dreams, though he at first resists the understanding of his own being that they offer him:

> Great watery spaces opened out before me, and I seemed to wander through titanic sunken porticoes and labyrinths of reedy Cyclopean walls with grotesque fishes as my companions. Then the other shapes began to appear, filling me with nameless horror the moment I awoke. But during the dreams they did not horrify me at all—I was one with them; wearing their unhuman trappings, treading their aqueous ways, and praying monstrously at their evil sea-bottom temples. (651)

There was, the narrator claims, "much more than he could remember" to his dreams, and, as they persist, the balance between conscious horror and unconscious pleasure in his response to them begins to shift. He feels himself "queerly drawn toward the unknown sea-deeps instead of fearing them," and awakens "with a kind of exaltation instead of terror" (652–53). Like all Lovecraft's fantasias of nonhuman architecture, the "phosphorescent palace of many terraces" in which his narrator encounters the grandmother who can at last be acknowledged as his ancestor, strikes a careful balance between the historical and the fantastic: its walls are Cyclopean both in the way that the architecture of early Greece is properly so called, and in the way that such remains, like the remnants of Roman architecture in the Old English poem "The Ruin," have been imagined as the work of nonhuman builders.

45. Memory and pseudo-memory, as they relate to human beings' ability to access the millennia of prehuman existence in dream, are explored at length in Lovecraft's "The Shadow Out of Time."

As such, Lovecraft's palace belongs to myth's archive of gods' underwater homes: the palace of Poseidon in which Theseus is dressed and adorned by the sea goddess Amphitrite in Bacchylides' seventeenth Ode; the house of the river god Achelous, with its walls of pumice stone, moss floor, and ceiling paneled with purple shells in Ovid's *Metamorphoses* (8.562–65); the hall below the mere, bedecked with the weapons of conquered heroes, in which Beowulf encounters the mother of the monster Grendel whose arm he has nailed to the wall of the human hall Heorot in the world above. What Lovecraft's tale wants to tell us, however, is that these submarine palaces are really memories, memories of the lives our bodies used to lead when they belonged to beings different in form from the ones who inhabit them now, and which are preserved in garbled form in the tissues of the animal they have become.

In Lovecraft's fantasy of evolutionary memory, the human being is an animal that resists knowing what it is: its narrator refuses to accept the true history of his own body until this knowledge is forced upon him by a literal metamorphosis of his body at the hands of superior beings. As Aristophanes put it in *Birds*, "by words the mind is lifted to the clouds, and humankind is exalted" [ὑπὸ γὰρ λόγων ὁ νοῦς τε μετεωρίζεται ἐπαίρεται τ' ἄνθρωπος] (1447). It is only with difficulty that human beings can talk themselves down from the lofty perch to which they have raised themselves.[46]

Lovecraft's blend of evolutionary knowledge, fantasies of divine power, and tropes of literary metamorphosis suggests that a single human desire is invested in all three, namely, a will to imagine a force outside the human subject that has the power to transform its body without the owner's consent.[47] Rosi Braidotti has called foreclosure of the autonomous development of somatic experience by an agent external to the developing subject "ontological kidnapping,"[48] and a version of such foreclosure, in which God has the

46. "The Shadow Over Innsmouth" is a good example of what Morton calls "dark ecology," ways of writing human being that point to the thick walls and lack of illumination in "the prison of the beautiful soul" human beings have fashioned for themselves by staging the degree of difficulty they experience in emerging from it (2007, 140–43).

47. Dawkins (2006, 2–3, 267–68) points out how consistently the genome has been misconstrued as a power antagonistic to human will; see, for example, Midgley (1985, 124–33).

48. Braidotti (2002, 45), referring to the foreclosure of the homosexual body in normative childrearing and its psychoanalytic justifications, from which the subject may fashion a psychic escape in metamorphosis, especially the Deleuzian "becoming animal" in which the pack or swarm, not the individual body—a prisoner of the developmental narratives that have hijacked it, like the nipple and thumb of evolutionary history—is the proper threshold of experience (262).

power to remake a person unable to better himself through his own efforts, has always been a province of devotional literature: Donne's "Batter my heart, three person'd God," with its plea to God to "break, blow, burn and make me new" is a celebrated example.

Fantasies of life-altering transformation visited upon a human being by an all-powerful outsider are clearly continuous with the divinely initiated metamorphosis stories of pagan literature. More surprisingly, perhaps, human beings are able to experience their actual development, both ontogenetically and phylogenetically, as the work of a power whose shaping force feels external to them. The life biologists call autopoiesis can feel heteropoietic to its subjects,[49] and the sense this feeling fosters that the human body might have been made other than it is nourishes the regret for lost possibilities enacted in narratives of failed human efforts to participate in the lives of other organisms.

Compare the story of Peisetairus and Euelpides with the protreptic to natural history by Darwin's great imaginative exponent Charles Kingsley: *Glaucus; Or, the Wonders of the Shore.*[50] Kingsley veers wildly between the desire to become part of the underwater world of the organisms he studies, as this desire is so wonderfully realized in Ovid's tale of the fisherman's transformation, and the sense that renunciation of this desire is adequately compensated by the scientific knowledge it enables.[51] The naturalist of *Glaucus* longs for the transformation that Tom, the child hero of *The Water-Babies* experiences unwilled, but he knows that only in art can a person become "a companion of the fair semi-human forms with which the Hellenic poets peopled their sunny bays and firths" (71). Desire for what is nonhuman, and the understanding of what is nonhuman, must be satisfied by different pursuits.

But what of a Nature that, in Donna Haraway's phrase, has been made

49. On autopoiesis as an organism's self-unfolding in response to changing circumstances, see Margulis (1986, 66); on this effort as analogous to Spinoza's concept of *conatus*, see Margulis and Sagan (1995, 44). Beer (1983, 107–8) cites Virginia Woolf on the child's sense that its growth is authored by someone, or something, other than itself: "One must get the feeling that made her press on, the little creature driven on as she was by growth of her legs and arms, driven without her being able to stop it, or to change it, driven as a plant is driven up out of the earth, up until the stalk grows, the leaf grows, buds swell." At the species level, Dawkins (1986, xviii) wonders why the human brain appears "specifically designed to misunderstand Darwinism, and find it hard to believe."

50. Kingsley was the only recipient of a signed and inscribed prepublication copy of *The Origin of Species*; see Kinglsey (2008, xii).

51. See Kingsley (1890, 45). Beer (1983, 132) records that Darwin's children informed him that his eulogistic description of the cirripede larva sounded like an advertisement.

"fully artifactual" by the progress of genetic science?[52] How would Kingsley's inner clergyman have responded to the news that the ontological creativity of ancient poets is now within the grasp of modern engineers? The divinity of this world is clearly not the distant non-interventionist of Donne's poem, only to be called upon for serious business. It is more like the whimsical Eros of antiquity, whose power is no less awesome because it can be discerned everywhere in the world around us.[53] What can we expect from this as yet somewhat unknown god?

One possibility is the satisfaction of Kingsley's desires in designer ecosystems populated by the mythological hybrids of world literature and/or whatever large animals human beings might want to keep around. Their friendliness to humankind will have been genetically guaranteed, and such creatures, it has been suggested, will be "no more or less soulful than animals currently residing in the San Diego Zoo."[54] But what of us, we other animals, for whom these wonders will have been wrought? How soulful will we be? How much do we really know about the desires that a world remade in their image is intended to appease? Might we not linger a while longer with our fascination by what is other than ourselves before we decide that the best way to satisfy it is a world of our own creations that will everywhere and exclusively reflect our own image back to us?

52. Haraway 1997, 108.
53. As Clarke observes, "narratives of bodily transformation are nonmodern—at once archaic and posthuman" (2008, 193), and eros is, as in antiquity, the force behind them (51).
54. Silver 2007, 309–14.

I Do Not Know What It Is
I Am Like

The water-bug's mittens show on the bright rock below him.
—Ezra Pound, addendum for *Canto* C

There are good reasons for thinking that new regimes of desire are coming to occupy the contact zone between human beings and other animals. Not only are the complexities of social interaction in animals once taken as the purest instantiations of wildness—wolves and whales, for example—being charted, but modes of sociality are themselves increasingly being shown to be amenable to the same kind of genomic intervention as an organism's physical characteristics.[1] When human beings no longer understand their encounters with other animals as a meeting between nature and culture, how will they experience them?

Bill Viola's video *I Do Not Know What It Is I Am Like* is a work that thematizes the suspension of knowledge in encounters with other animals. It consists of five parts: "Il Corpo Scuro (The Dark Body)," "The Language of the Birds," "The Night of Sense," "Stunned by the Drum," and "The Living Flame." A narrative summary might go something like this: the video begins with sideways shots of mountains, pine trees, and the sky above them, filmed by a camera submerged in water. Then it cuts to a cave whose mineral surfaces look like human tissue (they are wet orange, pink, and brown). Then flies swarm noisily on the carcass of a bison as other bison stand grazing in an

---

1. See Silver (2007, 74–75), for example, on monogamy artificially induced in the meadow vole.

upland meadow against a backdrop of quiet lightning. One urinates at length, the sky reflected in his eye. Next, lamps float in a river as part of a religious ceremony, and huge, richly colored birds' eyes fill the screen. The video camera is reflected in the pupil of an owl, and then we see the video maker at home, at night, editing the images we have just witnessed. A cry is heard that could be a baby or a cat. From a silver platter, a hand takes cooked fish and bread, accompanied by noisy crunching. A snail emerges from its shell and a chick hatches from an egg. An elephant picks up a coffee cup and stands in the room, which is now brightly illuminated. There are more fire ceremonies, interspersed with attack dogs bounding at the camera. The mountain landscape returns, a fish is superimposed on aerial shots of rivers and forests then lies on the ground by a lake, melting away in time lapse, its body consumed by birds and flies.

Viola described the video as "a personal investigation of the inner states and connections to animal consciousness we all carry within,"[2] and the video produces such a full spectrum of such states and connections that its effect is almost bewildering in its plurality: a stunning parade of biodiversity in the sequence of birds' eyes that is like the wonder of Aristophanes' *Birds* in close-up; the sublime fury of angry dogs that recalls the iambic poets' flights into nonhuman aggression; the awareness of shared physiological process that dawns on the viewer in the bison sequence, and its denial in human consumption of animal flesh; the feeling of impossible, quasi-divine knowledge we get from watching a fish's body decompose in a camera angle and period of time no human subject could sustain; the difficulty we experience in distinguishing the cry of an animal from the wail of a child.

In addition to its catalogic qualities, Viola's video thematizes the work of its own production. In the end credits, we learn that the video maker has been an artist-in-residence at the San Diego Zoo (the birds that feature in the video are named and identified by species, as is Nita, the elephant) and that parts of the video were shot at Mahadevi Temple in Fiji, Jewel Cave National Monument, and Wind Cave National Park, South Dakota (known for its free range bison as well as for its cave). More than expressions of gratitude for support, these notices characterize the video as a record of actual observation, time spent getting to know its subjects at first hand.

The acknowledgment of *historia* in the credits is complemented by the disclosure of *poiesis* that appears in the video itself as the work of editing.

---

2. Copies can be rented from Electronic Arts Intermix (http://www.eai.org), where this description is cited.

Marjorie Perloff, in her discussion of *I Do Not Know What It Is I Am Like*, cites a 1981 statement by the artist in which he emphasizes video's "roots in the live." A video camera, Viola argues, more closely resembles a microphone in its operation than a film camera, because it receives input from its environment constantly, and what it records is truly an ongoing process and not a succession of still images. The video artist's work lies in deciding what to leave out, as he shapes a specific thing from a recording whose content he has not determined in advance, and not in the framing, arrangement, and structuring that decide what the image will be prior to its registration.

Perloff uses this claim to investigate what Viola means by calling his work "poetic," and she finds an answer in Plato's *Ion*, claiming that, for Viola, "art is a form of practical knowledge . . . *techne kai episteme*."[3] Viola's work certainly belongs with the lyric poetry of Gerard Manley Hopkins and Ezra Pound in its desire to disclose something about other animals directly, without using the modes of sympathetic identification enabled by narrative fiction. It cannot, however, be described as *techne*, in Plato's sense of this term, for *I Do Not Know What It Is I Am Like* turns away from the effort to know what it is that we encounter in other animals, and interrogates instead the loss of presumptive understanding that occurs in these meetings, "letting knowledge come to an end," as Stanley Cavell has recommended.[4]

The video's end credits give us the source for its title in *Rig Veda* (1.164.37), and it is helpful in understanding Viola's project to see this citation in the full context of the hymn, which I give here in two translations: "What thing I truly am I know not clearly: mysterious, fettered in my mind I wander" (Griffith); "I do not know just what it is that I am like. I wander about concealed and wrapped in thought" (Doniger).[5] For the hymn poet, everyday human thinking is a kind of impairment: a wrapper, obstacle, or fetter that blocks the human subject from the fuller forms of understanding that emerge from encounters with the nonhuman. This cloud that conceals human being from itself is dispersed by the eye, the breath, the bark of the other in cognitive events that are both subject specific and a generalizable possibility for renewed human understanding: "personal investigation of the inner states and connections to animal consciousness we all carry within."

3. Perloff 1998, 312–13.
4. In a letter to Vicki Hearne, cited by Wolfe (2003b, 5).
5. Griffith's translation can be found at the Internet Sacred Text Archive (http://www .sacred-texts.com), and, with links to the concordance, at IntraText (http://www.intratext .com); Doniger's in Doniger (1981, 71–83).

This book began with a beaver in the woods of northern Michigan—a likely enough place to meet with one. It ends with a fish in the Nevada desert. Just outside Las Vegas, in the Ash Meadows National Wildlife Refuge, a detached unit of Death Valley National Park, there is a crack in the earth four hundred feet deep that goes by the name of Devils Hole. At the bottom of this hole there is water—a small aquifer-fed pool, typically around ninety degrees Fahrenheit— and in this water live Devils Hole pupfish. They are bright blue and a little less than one inch long, and they have lived in this pool and nowhere else for something like twenty thousand years—ever since the lake that covered Death Valley receded at the end of the last ice age, stranding them in their tiny oasis.

When I visited Devils Hole in the early 1990s, I peered over the railing into the cavern but could not catch a glimpse of the fish in the darkness below. It was hardly the kind of wildlife experience that seems destined to leave a permanent trace in the imagination. And yet for some reason I never stopped thinking about the Devils Hole pupfish. Their unlikely name probably had something to do with it—it was funny to imagine a fish that might somehow act like a puppy—but mostly what stuck in my mind was the thought of their longevity: how the world up above had changed, as the pupfish lingered on in their desert cavern.

When my colleague Richard Strier read an earlier version of this book, he brought to my attention the Supreme Court case that pitted the Tennessee Valley Authority against environmentalists who wished to save a small fish called the snail darter (*TVA v. Hill*, 437 U.S. 153 [1978]): the building of the Tellico Dam on the Little Tennessee River promised to destroy what appeared to be its only habitat and so wipe out the species. Tellico was given an exemption from the Endangered Species Act, allowing the dam to be built. The river was destroyed, but the snail darter was saved: some fish were transferred to another river, and they have since been discovered in other locations. Richard did not know this when he told me about the case, and he wrote: "I mourn the loss of the snail darter (which, of course, I've never seen). The chain of being seems damaged to me."

Like my fascination with the pupfish, Richard's concern for the snail darter was a matter of imaginative understanding: once you know they exist, they become a small but indispensable part of the world in which you feel yourself to be living.[6] This is how Theodore Roosevelt understood the satisfaction

---

6. The Devils Hole pupfish was one of the first species protected under the Endangered Species Act. Their fortunes can be followed at http://www.fws.gov/Nevada/protected_species/fish/species/dhp/dhp.html.

human beings get from what we have come to call biodiversity, the pleasure in being surrounded by an abundance of other species, and the pain we suffer in their diminishment:

> I do not understand how any man or woman who really loves nature can fail to try to exert all influence in support of such objects as those of the Audubon Society. Spring would not be spring without bird songs, any more than it would be spring without buds and flowers, and I only wish that besides protecting the songsters, the birds of the grove, the orchard, the garden and the meadow, we could also protect the birds of the sea-shore and of the wilderness . . . How immensely it would add to our forests if the great Logcock were still found among them! The destruction of the Wild Pigeon and the Carolina Paroquet has meant a loss as severe as if the Catskills or the Palisades were taken away. When I hear of the destruction of a species I feel just as if the works of some great writer had perished; as if we had lost all instead of only part of Polybius or Livy.[7]

Roosevelt's analogy between the irreplaceability of the achievements of human culture and the irreplaceability of animal species involves a set of finely differentiated feelings. There is mourning for what has been lost: the pain of knowing we have only a few fragments of the poetry of Sappho, only a handful of the plays of Sophocles, instead of the full richness of everything they wrote. And there is the consolation of imagining the vanished plenitude from the remnants that we have. This is how we think about bison: they may no longer roam freely over the Great Plains, but we can still see a few of them and picture what it was like when they "shook their iron manes" from Illinois to Montana.

In the case of the passenger pigeon or the Carolina parakeet, however, it is as if we were to try to imagine the works of Sappho from some Byzantine grammarian's description of them: when what is irreplaceable is lost, it becomes unimaginable. Richard Leakey cites Julian Simon's skepticism regarding the human value of the loss of species that occurred when settlers clear-cut the forests of the Midwest: "It seems hard to even *imagine* that we would be enormously better off with the persistence of any such imagined species."[8] But this is, in fact, exactly what Roosevelt is claiming: when species

7. Roosevelt 1951, 948.
8. Leakey 1995, 247.

are extinct, we cannot even imagine what is lost to us with their disappearance. To grasp the ramifications of his analogy between the ecology of living things and the ecology of the human imagination is to come again to a version of Gerard Manley Hopkins's vicious circle. You can imagine a world without bison or without Sappho only because there are still bison and still some fragments of Sappho; you can no more imagine a world without the passenger pigeon, or without some Greek poet who is only a name to us, than you can imagine a world with them.

Since the possibilities for human self-understanding that other animals enable emerge unpredictably from encounters with their living presence, there is no way of knowing in advance what human beings stand to lose from their disappearance. As Melville never tires of reminding his readers, *Moby-Dick* is unlike all the books ever written about whales by people who had never been in their presence, and, given the perilous state to which the sperm whale population had been reduced in his time, he came close to being denied this opportunity himself. If we feel that our human world might not lose all that much with the extinction of some obscure species or another, we might pause for a moment to consider what that world would be like without *Moby-Dick*.[9]

I did not see a pupfish when I stared into their cavern in the Nevada desert, but I knew they were down there somewhere, and I was free to think about them, or not. Some part of me chose to, and while I may not have learned to think like a desert, I did learn to think about the desert—to dwell within the thought of what goes on without human beings in such secret places of the earth. Recall William Carlos Williams's Aztec grasshopper, a "matt stone solicitously instructed | to bear away some rumor | of the living presence that has preceded | it." The sculpture from Chapultepec pays homage to an animal that has enabled the human mind to get beyond itself. It is what allows Williams to say of love itself that it is "a stone endlessly in flight." Do we need as many miraculous stones as there are species among whom we wish to dwell? Perhaps not, but, as Roosevelt saw clearly, conservation requires men and women who love nature if the work of scientifically informed legislators is to endure. There are, of course, many ways, and many places, in which such love can be born, but art is not the least, nor the least effective, among them.

9. So Silver points to the growing need for emotional and imaginative arguments for the preservation of other species and their habitats now that the useful medications it was once argued awaited discovery in them are ever more easily synthesized from scratch in the laboratory (2007, 306–313).

Its rumors of living presence strike hard, and they provoke lasting curiosity about the things of the world that have inspired them. No doubt a novel about an inch-long blue fish that lives its entire life in a hole in the floor of the Nevada desert is hard to imagine, but, then again, so is a novel about a huge white whale that roams the South Pacific.

REFERENCES

Allen, D. 2000. *The world of Prometheus.* Princeton, NJ.

Altieri, C. 2001. "Lyrical ethics and literary experience." In Davis and Wornack 2001, 30–58.

———. 2003. *The particulars of rapture.* Ithaca, NY.

Ambler, W. H. "Aristotle's understanding of the naturalness of the city." *Review of Politics* 47:163–85.

Ardrey, R. 1966. *The territorial imperative.* New York.

Armstrong, P. 2004. "'Leviathan is a skein of networks': Translations of nature and culture in *Moby-Dick.*" *English Literary History* 71:1039–63.

Arnhart, L. 1994. "The Darwinian biology of Aristotle's political animals." *American Journal of Political Science* 38:464–85.

Arrowsmith, W. 1973. "Aristophanes' *Birds*: The fantasy politics of Eros." *Arion* 1:119–67.

Ausband, S. C. 1975. "The whale and the machine: An approach to *Moby-Dick.*" *American Literature* 47:197–211.

Baker, J. A. 1967. *The peregrine.* New York. Repr., with introd. by Robert Macfarlane, New York Review Books, 2005.

Ballinger, P. A. 2000. *The poem as sacrament.* Louvain, Belgium.

Bartley, A. N. 2003. *Stories from the mountains, stories from the sea.* Göttingen.

Bartol, K. 1993. *Greek elegy and iambus.* Poznán, Poland.

Bateson, G. 1972. *Steps to an ecology of mind.* New York.

Beer, G. 1983. *Darwin's plots.* London.

Bell, I. F. A. 1981. *Critic as scientist.* London.

Bell, J. M. 1984. "God, man, and animal in Pindar's second *Pythian.*" In *Greek poetry and philosophy: Studies in honor of Leonard Woodbury,* ed. D. E. Gerber, 1–32. Chico, CA.

Bernasconi, R., and D. Wood, eds. 1988. *The provocation of Lévinas*. London.

Bernstein, M. A. 1992. *Bitter carnival*. Princeton, NJ.

Booth, W. 2001. "Why ethical criticism can never be simple." In Davis and Wornack 2001, 16–29.

Braidotti, R. 2002. *Metamorphosis*. Cambridge.

Bremen, B. A. 1993. *William Carlos Williams and the diagnostics of culture*. New York.

Breslin, J. E. B. 1970. *William Carlos Williams: An American artist*. Chicago.

Brown, C. G. 1997. "Iambos." In *A companion to the Greek lyric poets*, ed. D. E. Gerber, 11–88. Leiden, the Netherlands.

———. 2006. "Pindar on Archilochus and the gluttony of blame (*Pyth.* 2.52–6)." *Journal of Hellenic Studies* 126:36–46.

Buell, L. 2001. *Writing for an endangered world*. Cambridge, MA.

Burkert, W. 1983. *Homo necans*. Berkeley, CA.

Burnett, A. P. 1983. *Three archaic poets*. Cambridge, MA.

Burnett, D. G. 2007. *Trying Leviathan*. Princeton, NJ.

Bush, R. 1999. "Late cantos." In Nadel 1999, 109–38.

Calarco, M. 2004. "Deconstruction is not vegetarianism: Humanism, subjectivity, and animal ethics." *Continental Philosophy Review* 37:175–201.

Calarco, M., and P. Atterton, eds. 2004. *Animal philosophy*. London.

Callan, R. 1992. *William Carlos Williams and transcendentalism*. New York.

Calloway, C. G. 1996. *Our hearts fell to the ground*. Boston.

Capponi, F. 1972. *P. Ovidii Nasonis Halieuticon*. 2 vols. Leiden, the Netherlands.

Carson, R. 1986. *Under the sea-wind*. New York.

Cavell, S. 1979. *The claim of reason*. Oxford.

Ceccarelli, P. 2000. "Life among the savages and escape from the city." In Harvey and Wilkins 2000, 453–72.

Céline, L.-F. 1997. *Rigadoon*. Normal, IL.

———. 1999. *Ballets without music, without dancers, without anything*. Copenhagen.

———. 2006. *Conversations with Professor Y*. Normal, IL.

Clark, M. M. 2004. "Art and suffering in two late poems by William Carlos Williams." *Literature and Medicine* 23:226–40.

Clarke, B. 2008. *Posthuman metamorphosis*. New York.

Clay, D. 2004. *Archilochus heros*. Washington DC.

Coetzee, J. M. 2003. *Elizabeth Costello*. New York.

Cooper, J. M. 2005. "Political animals and civic friendship." In *Aristotle's* Politics: *Critical essays*, ed. R. Kraut and S. Skultety, 65–90. Lanham, MD.

Couser, G. T. 2004. *Vulnerable subjects*. Ithaca, NY.

Csapo, E. 1993a. "Deep ambivalence: Notes on a Greek cockfight. Part 1." *Phoenix* 47:1–28.

———. 1993b. "Deep ambivalence: Notes on a Greek cockfight. Part 2." *Phoenix* 47:115–24.

Cushman, S. 1985. *William Carlos Williams and the meanings of measure*. New Haven, CT.

Daitz, S. G. 1997. "Les voix d'animaux chez Aristophane." In Thiercy and Menu 1997, 309–16.

Darrieussecq, M. 1997. *Pig tales*. New York.

Davis, T. F., and K. Wornack, eds. 2001. *Mapping the ethical turn*. Charlottesville, VA.

Dawkins, R. 1986. *The blind watchmaker*. New York.

———. 2006. *The selfish gene*. 30th anniversary ed. Oxford.

Day, B. J. 2004. "Hopkins' spiritual ecology in 'Binsey Poplars.'" *Victorian Poetry* 42:181–93.

Deleuze, G., and F. Guattari. 1986. *Kafka*. Minneapolis, MN.

Depew, D. J. 1995. "Humans and other political animals in Aristotle's *History of animals*." *Phronesis* 40:156–81.

Derrida, J. 1991. "'Eating well,' or the calculation of the subject: An interview with Jacques Derrida." In *Who comes after the subject?* ed. E. Cadava, P. Connor, and J.-L. Nancy, 96–119. New York.

———. 1992. "How to avoid speaking denials." In *Derrida and negative theology*, ed. H. Coward and T. Foshay, 73–142. Albany, NY.

———. 2002. "The animal that therefore I am (more to follow)." *Critical Inquiry* 28:369–418.

Diamond, J. 1992. *The third chimpanzee*. New York.

Doležel, L. 1990. *Occidental poetics*. Lincoln, NE.

———. 1998. *Heterocosmica*. Baltimore.

Doniger, W., trans. 1981. *The Rig Veda*. London.

———. 1988. *Other peoples' myths*. New York.

Dunbar, N. 1997. "Aristophane, ornithophile et ornithophage." In Thiercy and Menu 1997, 112–29.

———, ed. 1998. *Aristophanes: Birds*. Oxford.

Eakin, P. J. 1992. *Touching the world*. Princeton, NJ.

Elden, S. 2006. "Heidegger's animals." *Continental Philosophy Review* 39:273–91.

Empson, W. 1989. *The structure of complex words*. Cambridge, MA.

Evans, K. L. 2003. *Whale!* Minneapolis, MN.

Fantham, E. 2004. *Ovid's* Metamorphoses. Oxford.

Farrell, J. 1999. "The Ovidian *corpus*: Poetic body and poetic text." In Hardie, Barchiesi, and Hinds 1999, 127–41.

Feldherr, A. 2002. "Metamorphosis in the *Metamorphoses*." In *The Cambridge companion to Ovid*, ed. P. Hardie, 163–79. Cambridge.

Flaubert, G. 1961. *Three Tales*. London.

———. 1997. *Selected letters*. London.

Foley, H. 2000. "The comic body in Greek art and drama." In *Not the classical ideal*, ed. B. Cohen, 275–311. Leiden, the Netherlands.

Forbes Irving, P. M. C. 1990. *Metamorphosis in Greek myths*. Oxford.

Fränkel, H. 1945. *Ovid: A poet between two worlds.* Berkeley, CA.

French, R. 1994. *Ancient natural history.* London.

Fromm, E. 1973. *The anatomy of human destructiveness.* New York.

Galinsky, K. 1975. *Ovid's* Metamorphoses. Berkeley, CA.

———. 1998. "The Speech of Pythagoras at Ovid *Metamorphoses* 15.75-478." *Papers of the Leeds Latin Seminar* 10:313-36.

Gildenhard, I., and A. Zissos. 1999. "Somatic economies: Tragic bodies and poetic design in Ovid's *Metamorphoses.*" In Hardie, Barchiesi, and Hinds 1999, 162-81.

Gilhus, I. S. 2006. *Animals, gods, and humans.* New York.

Ginsberg, A. 2006. *Collected Poems, 1947-1997.* New York.

Halliwell, S., ed. 1987. *The* Poetics *of Aristotle.* Chapel Hill, NC.

Hammermeister, K. 2002. *The German aesthetic tradition.* Cambridge.

Haraway, D. 1997. *Modest_witness@second_millenium.* New York.

———. 2008. *When species meet.* Minneapolis, MN.

Hardie, P. 1995. "The speech of Pythagoras in Ovid's *Metamorphoses* 15: Empedoclean Epos." *Classical Quarterly* 45:204-14.

———. 2002. *Ovid's poetics of illusion.* Cambridge.

Hardie, P., A. Barchiesi, and S. Hinds, eds. 1999. *Ovidian Transformations: Essays on Ovid's* Metamorphoses *and its reception.* Cambridge.

Harrison, R. P. 1992. *Forests.* Chicago.

———. 2008. *Gardens.* Chicago.

Harvey, D., and J. Wilkins, eds. 2000. *The rivals of Aristophanes.* London.

Heath, J. 2005. *The talking Greeks.* Cambridge.

Heidegger, M. 1971. *Poetry, language, thought.* New York.

———. 1977a. *The question concerning technology and other essays.* New York.

———. 1977b. *Basic writings.* San Francisco.

Hemingway, E. 1986. *The garden of Eden.* New York.

———. 1987. *The complete short stories of Ernest Hemingway.* New York.

Hopkins, G. M. 1953. *Poems and prose.* Harmondsworth, UK.

———. 1991. *Selected letters.* Oxford.

Houellebecq, M. 2005. *H. P. Lovecraft.* San Francisco.

Howe, S. 1987. *Articulation of sound forms in time.* Windsor, VT.

Hubbard, T. K. 1994. "Elemental psychology and the date of Semonides of Amorgos." *American Journal of Philology* 115:175-97.

Ingold, T. 1988. "The animal in the study of humanity." In *What is an animal?* ed. T. Ingold, 84-99. New York.

Isenberg, A. C. 2000. *The destruction of the bison.* Cambridge.

Kahn, C. H. 1979. *The art and thought of Heraclitus.* Cambridge.

Kakridis, J. T. 1962. "Zum Weiberiambus des Semonides." *Wiener humanistische Blätter* 5:3-10.

Kellert, S. R., and E. O. Wilson, eds. 1993. *The biophilia hypothesis.* Washington DC.

Kingsley, C. 1890. *Glaucus: Or, the wonders of the shore.* London.

————. 2008. *The water-babies*. New York.

Klinkenborg, V. 2006. *Timothy: Or, notes of an abject reptile*. New York.

Kristeva, J. 1982. *Powers of horror*. New York.

Kroodsma, D. 2005. *The singing life of birds*. Boston.

Kullman, W. 1991. "Man as a political animal in Aristotle." In *A companion to Aristotle's* Politics, ed. D. Keyt and F. D. Miller Jr., 94–117. Oxford.

Kuzniar, A. A. 2006. *Melancholia's dog*. Chicago.

Lan, F. 2005. *Ezra Pound and Confucianism*. Toronto.

Latour, B. 1993. *We have never been modern*. Cambridge, MA.

Leakey, R. 1995. *The sixth extinction*. New York.

LeClair, T. 1970. "The poet as dog in *Paterson*." *Twentieth Century Literature* 16:97–108.

Lennox, J. G. 1999. "The place of mankind in Aristotle's zoology." *Philosophical Topics* 27:1–16.

Leopold, A. 1949. *A sand county almanac*. London.

Levaniouk, O. 1999. "Penelope and the *pênelops*." In *Nine essays on Homer*, ed. M. Carlisle and O. Levaniouk, 95–136. Lanham, MD.

Lévinas, E. 1981. *Otherwise than being*. Pittsburgh.

————. 1988. "The paradox of morality: An interview with Emmanuel Lévinas." In Bernasconi and Wood 1988, 168–80.

Lippit, A. M. 2000. *Electric animal*. Minneapolis, MN.

Lloyd, G. E. R. 1987. "Empirical research in Aristotle's biology." In *Philosophical issues in Aristotle's biology*, ed. A. Gotthelf and J. G. Lennox, 53–68, Cambridge.

————. 1991. "The invention of nature." In *Methods and problems in Greek science*, 417–34. Cambridge.

Lloyd-Jones, H. 1975. *Females of the species*. Park Ridge, NJ.

Loraux, N. 1993. "On the race of women and some of its tribes: Hesiod and Semonides." In *The children of Athena*, 72–110. Princeton, NJ.

Lovecraft, H. P. 2005. *Tales*. New York.

Lowell, R. 1972. "Thomas, Bishop and Williams." In Tomlinson 1972, 158–62.

Malamud, R. 2003. *Poetic animals and animal souls*. New York.

Malouf, D. 1978. *An imaginary life*. New York.

Margulis, L. 1986. *Microcosmos*. Berkeley, CA.

Margulis, L., and D. Sagan. 1995. *What is life?* Berkeley, CA.

Markos, D. W. 1994. *Ideas in things*. Cranbury, NJ.

Marx, L. 1964. *The machine in the garden*. London.

Melville, H. 1972. *Moby-Dick*. Harmondsworth, UK.

Midgley, M. 1985. *Evolution as a religion*. London.

Mikkelsen, A. 2003. "'The truth about us': Pastoral, pragmatism, and *Paterson*." *American Literature* 75:601–27.

Miller, A. M. 1981. "Pindar, Archilochus and Hieron in *P*. 2.52–56." *Transactions of the American Philological Association* 111:135–43.

Mills, C. 2004. "Friendship, fiction, and memoir: Trust and betrayal in writing from one's own life." In *The ethics of life writing*, ed. P. J. Eakin, 101–20. Ithaca, NY.

Morgan, T, 2005. "The wisdom of Semonides Fr. 7." *Proceedings of the Cambridge Philological Society* 51:72–85.

Morton, T. 2007. *Ecology without nature*. Cambridge, MA.

Nadel, I. B., ed. 1999. *The Cambridge companion to Ezra Pound*. Cambridge.

Naess, A. 1989. *Ecology, community and lifestyle*. Cambridge.

———. 2002. *Life's philosophy*. Athens, GA.

Nagel, T. 1974. "What is it like to be a bat?" *Philosophical Review* 83:435–50.

Nagy, G. 1979. *The best of the Achaeans*. Baltimore.

Nicholsen, S. W. 2002. *The love of nature and the end of the world*. Cambridge, MA.

Nussbaum, M. 1990. "'Finely aware and richly responsible': Literature and the moral imagination." In *Love's knowledge*, 148–67. Oxford.

Orr, D. W. 1993. "Love it or lose it: The coming biophilia revolution." In Kellert and Wilson 1993, 415–40.

Osborne, R. 2001. "The use of abuse: Semonides 7." *Proceedings of the Cambridge Philological Society* 47:47–64.

Padel, R. 1992. *In and out of the mind*. Princeton, NJ.

Parker, L. P. E. 1997. *The songs of Aristophanes*. Oxford.

Payne, M. 2007. *Theocritus and the invention of fiction*. Cambridge.

Pellizer, E., and G. Tedeschi. 1990. *Semonides: Testimonia et fragmenta*. Rome.

Perkell, C. 1993. "On the two voices of the birds in *Birds*." *Ramus* 22:1–18.

Perloff, M. 1998. *Poetry on and off the page*. Evanston, IL.

Pound, E. 1947. *Confucius*. New York.

———. 1975. *Selected prose: 1909–1965*. New York.

———. 1996. *The cantos*. New York.

Preus, A. 1975. *Science and philosophy in Aristotle's biological works*. Hildesheim, Germany.

Rakosi, C. 1986. *Collected poems*. Orono, ME.

Read, F. 1957. "The pattern of the Pisan *Cantos*." *Sewanee Review* 65:408–19.

Redfield, J. M. 1994. *Nature and culture in the* Iliad. Durham, NC.

Richmond, J. A. 1962. *The* Halieutica *ascribed to Ovid*. London.

Riddehough, G. B. 1959. "Man-into-beast changes in Ovid." *Phoenix* 13:201–9.

Riddel, J. N. 1974. *The inverted bell*. Baton Rouge, LA.

Romer, F. E. 1983. "When is a bird not a bird?" *Transactions of the American Philological Society* 113:135–42.

Roosevelt, T. 1951. *Letters*. Vol. 2. *1898–1900*. Cambridge, MA.

Rosen, R. 2007. *Making mockery*. Oxford.

Rothwell, K. S. Jr. 2007. *Nature, culture, and the origins of Greek comedy*. Cambridge.

Russo, L. 2004. *The forgotten revolution*. Berlin.

Saint-Denis, E. de. 1975. *Ovide: Halieutiques*. Paris.

Schear, L. 1984. "Semonides fr. 7: Wives and their husbands." *Echos du monde classique/Classical Views* 28:39–49.

Schiller, F. 1967. *On the aesthetic education of man.* Oxford.

Schultz, E. 2000. "Melville's environmental vision in *Moby-Dick.*" *Interdisciplinary Studies in Literature and Environment* 7:97–113.

Schuster, J. 2007. "William Carlos Williams, *Spring and All,* and the anthropological imaginary." *Journal of Modern Literature* 30:116–32.

Sheldon, L. 2002. "Messianic power and Satanic decay: Milton in *Moby-Dick.*" *Leviathan* 4:29–50.

Shepard, P. 1993. "On animal friends." In Kellert and Wilson 1993, 275–300.

Shubin, N. 2008. *Your inner fish.* New York.

Siebert, C. 2009. "Watching whales watching us." *New York Times Magazine,* July 12. http://www.nytimes.com/2009/07/12/magazine/12whales-t.html.

Sifakis, G. M. 1971. *Parabasis and animal choruses.* London.

Silver, L. 2007. *Challenging nature.* New York.

Slater, C. 1994. *Dance of the dolphin.* Chicago.

Slotkin, R. 1973. *Regeneration through violence.* Middletown, CT.

Smith, A. 2002. *The theory of the moral sentiments.* Cambridge.

Snell, B. 1982. *The discovery of the mind.* New York.

Sorabji, R. 1993. *Animal minds and human morals.* Ithaca, NY.

Steiner, D. 2001. *Images in mind.* Princeton, NJ.

———. 2002. "Indecorous dining, indecorous speech: Pindar's First *Olympian* and the poetics of consumption." *Arethusa* 35:297–314.

Stevens, W. 1957. *Opus posthumous.* New York.

Storey, I. C. 2003. *Eupolis: Poet of old comedy.* Oxford.

Symonds, J. A. 1880. *Studies of the Greek poets.* 2 vols. New York.

Tapscott, S. 1984. *American beauty.* New York.

Taylor, R. 1999. "The texts of the *Cantos.*" In Nadel 1999, 161–87.

Tedlock, D., ed.. 1985. *Popol Vuh.* New York.

Terrell, C. F. 1984. *A companion to the cantos of Ezra Pound.* 2 vols. Berkeley, CA.

Theodorakopoulos, E. 1999. "Closure and transformation in Ovid's *Metamorphoses.*" In Hardie, Barchiesi, and Hinds 1999, 142–61.

Thiercy, P., and M. Menu. 1997. *Aristophane: La langue, la scène, la cité.* Bari, Italy.

Thoreau, H. 1985. *A Week on the Concord and Merrimack Rivers | Walden; Or, Life in the Woods | The Maine Woods | Cape Cod.* New York.

Tissol, G. 1997. *The face of nature.* Princeton, NJ.

Tomlinson, C. 1972. *William Carlos Williams.* Harmondsworth, UK.

Uther, H.-J. 2004. *The types of international folktales.* 3 vols. Helsinki.

Van Sickle, J. 1995. "The new erotic fragment of Archilochus." *Quaderni urbinati di cultura classica* 20:123–56.

Verdenius, W. J. 1968. "Semonides über die Frauen: Ein Kommentar zu fr. 7." *Mnemosyne* 21:132–58.

Vincent, H. P. 1949. *The trying-out of* Moby-Dick. Boston.

Von Hallberg, R. 1974. "Olson's relation to Pound and Williams." *Contemporary Literature* 15:15–48.

Wallace, D. F. 2006. *Consider the lobster and other essays*. New York.

Walton, K. L. 1990. *Mimesis as make-believe*. Cambridge, MA.

Watson, L. C. 1995. "Horace's epodes: The impotence of *iambos*?" In *Homage to Horace*, ed. S. J. Harrison, 188–202. Oxford.

West, M. L., ed. 1971. *Iambi et elegi Graeci ante Alexandrum cantati*. 2 vols. Oxford.

———. 1974. *Studies in Greek elegy and iambus*. Berlin.

———. 1982. *Greek metre*. Oxford.

Whitby, M. 2007. "The *Cynegetica* attributed to Oppian." In *Severan culture*, ed. S. Swain, S. Harrison, and J. Elsner, 125–34. Cambridge.

White, G. 1977. *The natural history of Selborne*. London.

Whitman, C. 1964. *Aristophanes and the comic hero*. Cambridge, MA.

Whitman, W. 1996. *Poetry and prose*. New York.

Wilkins, J. 2000a. "Edible choruses." In Harvey and Wilkins 2000, 341–54.

———. 2000b. *The boastful chef*. Oxford.

Williams, W. C. 1986–88. *Collected poems*. 2 vols. New York.

———. 1992. *Paterson*. New York.

Wilson, E. O. 1984. *Biophilia*. Cambridge, MA.

———. 1993. "Biophilia and the conservation ethic." In Kellert and Wilson 1993, 31–41.

———. 1998. *Consilience*. New York.

Wolfe, C. 2003a. "In the shadow of Wittgenstein's lion: Language, ethics, and the question of the animal." In *Zoontologies*, ed. C. Wolfe, 1–58. Minneapolis, MN.

———. 2003b. *Animal rites*. Chicago.

Wollheim, R. 1984. *The thread of life*. New Haven, CT.

Wordsworth, W. 1904. *Poetical works*. Oxford.

Zirin, R. A. 1980. "Aristotle's biology of language." *Transactions of the American Philological Association* 110:325–47.

Zoellner, R. 1973. *The salt-sea mastodon*. Berkeley, CA.

INDEX OF HUMANS

INDEX OF OTHER ANIMALS